D1410341

ECON

Quality Teaching

Reflection as the Heart of Practice

Joelle K. Jay

A SCARECROWEDUCATION BOOK

The Scarecrow Press, Inc.
Lanham, Maryland, and Oxford
2003

A SCARECROWEDUCATION BOOK

Published in the United States of America
by Scarecrow Press, Inc.
A Member of the Rowman & Littlefield Publishing Group
4501 Forbes Boulevard, Suite 200, Lanham, Maryland 20706
www.scarecroweducation.com

PO Box 317
Oxford
OX2 9RU, UK

Copyright © 2003 by Joelle Kristin Jay

All rights reserved. No part of this publication may be reproduced,
stored in a retrieval system, or transmitted in any form or by any
means, electronic, mechanical, photocopying, recording, or otherwise,
without the prior permission of the publisher.

British Library Cataloguing in Publication Information Available

Library of Congress Cataloging-in-Publication Data

Jay, Joelle Kristin.
  Quality teaching : reflection as the heart of practice /
Joelle K. Jay.
     p. cm.
  "A ScarecrowEducation book."
  Includes bibliographical references and index.
  ISBN 0-8108-4715-9 (pbk. : alk. paper)
  1. Teaching. 2. Reflection (Philosophy). I. Title.
LB1025.3.J39 2003
371.102—dc21

                                                    2002154949

∞™ The paper used in this publication meets the minimum requirements of
American National Standard for Information Sciences—Permanence of
Paper for Printed Library Materials, ANSI/NISO Z39.48-1992.
Manufactured in the United States of America.

For Tim

Contents

Acknowledgments   vii

Section 1:   Reflection as a Matter of Quality Teaching

1   Why Reflection Matters   1

2   Reflection in Teaching: Reviewing the Research   11

3   A Qualitative Case Study of Refection: Research Methods   24

Section 2:   Multiple Matters: Reflection in Schools

4   Reflecting in School: The Professional Context   35

5   Staff Meetings   41

6   Department Meetings   50

7   Informal Collegial Meetings   60

8   Teacher Evaluation   66

9   In the Context of Teaching   74

10   Reflection and the Conditions of Schools   83

Section 3:   Mind over Matter: Reflection in Programs

11   Reflecting in Programs: The Programmatic Context   92

12   The NBPTS Certification Process   99

13   A Voluntary Program for Teacher Assessment   113

14   Mentoring Programs   119

15   Reflection and the Conditions of Programs   127

Section 4:   The Heart of the Matter: Reflecting on One's Own

16   Reflecting on One's Own: The Personal Context   138

17   A Critical Friends Group   142

18   A Regional Conference   152

19   Quiet Spaces and Personal Places   163

20   The Conditions for Reflecting on One's Own   170

Section 5:   Discussion: What Matters in Teachers' Reflection

21   Lessons Learned Across Contexts   178

22   The Heart of Quality Teaching   195

References   205

Index   210

About the Author   216

Acknowledgments

I sincerely wish to thank the people who have supported me through the writing of this book. Nathalie Gehrke, Reed Stevens, Jerry Bamburg, George Dillon, and Bobbie Berkowitz were enormously helpful in guiding the research project. Because of them, the process was as inspiring as it was challenging.

My readers also deserve special mention: Amy Eva-Wood, Laura Adriance, Jennifer Joyce, and Jean Snell. Draft after draft, they sustained me with their thoughtfulness, interest, and friendship. Numerous other friends and colleagues also generously provided me with feedback, and I thank them!

I am profoundly grateful to the four teachers who participated in this project. Their commitment to the young people in their classrooms and to their own learning does honor to the profession of teaching. Among others, teachers Karen Kikolasy, John Traxler, and Nancy Miller are quoted throughout the book. It could not have been written without their insight and expertise.

I would also like to thank the hardworking editors at ScarecrowEducation. Thanks to them, the process of creating this book has been a pleasure.

Finally, I thank my parents, friends and family, whose love and belief in me have endured through this process and enriched my life along the way. Miki and David Trujillo and Mike and Shelly Lavin deserve special recognition for providing me with a quiet writing retreat. I especially thank my loving husband, Tim, who patiently saw me through this book from start to finish.

Chapter One

Why Reflection Matters

We should ridicule a merchant who said that he had sold a great many goods although no one had bought any. But perhaps there are teachers who think that they have done a good day's teaching irrespective of what [students] have learned

—John Dewey, *How We Think*

What counts as a "good day's teaching"? How do we know it when we see it? Despite efforts to quantify, grade, test, and otherwise assess teaching and learning, it remains difficult to tell on a daily basis whether students are actually buying the goods teachers offer. Unlike the merchant, who can count his wares to see how many have sold, teachers must approach self-evaluation more creatively. For many accomplished teachers acclaimed for the quality of their practice, to do so involves ongoing *reflection.*

Reflection means thinking about what one is doing. It entails a process of contemplation with an openness to being changed, a willingness to learn, and a sense of responsibility for doing one's best. Perhaps this process seems natural, and indeed it may be; but it also poses a challenge.

Consider a metaphor of "reflection." Think about looking at your reflection in a mirror and you'll get a sense of how easy it can be to "reflect," or to see an image shown back to you. Yet it is much more difficult to truly *look* at yourself. It can be painful to face your flaws, uncomfortable to acknowledge your strengths, and both odd and inspiring to glimpse yourself from another point of view. Such are the dualities of seeing your own reflection.

1

So it is with reflection in teaching. Reflective teachers face the challenge of truly seeing themselves and their teaching. They approach their practice with openness, wholeheartedness, and responsibility, looking for the better path to take, the edges that need to be smoothed, and the changes they need to make in their practice to improve learning for students. This is the heart of quality teaching.

Dewey (1933) says as much regarding the role of reflection in education: "The only way to increase the learning of students is to augment the quantity and quality of real teaching"(p. 36). In this simple idea, Dewey states the very essence of teaching and learning, exposing the essentials that really matter in education. Students learn when teachers teach well. But how do teachers know when they're teaching well? How can they be supported and encouraged to think about the quality of their teaching and its impact on student learning? These questions capture many present-day dilemmas about education and the professional learning of teachers. They also form the basis for this book. *Quality Teaching: Reflection as the Heart of Practice* explores a key element of quality teaching: teachers' reflection on their own practice. By studying the experiences of four accomplished teachers, we can learn about where, when, and how reflection informs teaching, what conditions support effective reflection, and how to minimize the barriers to reflective practice. Illustrations and examples drawn from these teachers' lives—representative samples from a larger body of research—form the basis of a rich and complex discussion about reflection in quality teaching. The book can be seen as an effort to discover more about the questions posed by Dewey's simple and seminal idea: improving students' learning by learning more about quality teaching.

A CONSENSUS IN THE RESEARCH

In the literature on effective education, one message is consistently clear: the most important influence on student learning is quality teaching (Darling-Hammond & Sykes, 1999. Correspondingly, researchers and policy makers alike are attending to the attributes of quality teaching, creating a virtual consensus as to the essential knowledge, skills, and dispositions for teachers

(Ball & Cohen, 1999; Hawley & Valli, 1999). Consistently, these discussions emphasize the importance of teachers' professional judgment—a judgment that arises out of a knowledgeable and thoughtful approach to teaching and the examination of practice by teachers themselves. One of the hallmarks of this kind of teaching is an ability to be reflective about practice—a central feature of growth and development in "the learning profession" (Darling-Hammond & Sykes, 1999).

Essential in a thoughtful approach to teaching, reflection represents one way teachers grow in and learn from their practice—a kind of experiential, ongoing learning well suited to the constantly changing world of the classroom. Importantly, reflection helps teachers develop "the capability and orientation to make informed and intelligent decisions about what to do, when to do it, and why it should be done" (Richert, 1990, p. 509). As is evident in the research and theory, reflection is a critical piece in effective teaching *and* teachers' learning. Yet, paradoxically, reflection often falls last in a long list of educational priorities, raising critical questions about how to support reflective practice in the busy and constantly changing world of education.

A NEW IMPERATIVE FOR EDUCATORS

General agreement about the importance of reflection in quality teaching creates a new imperative: to move beyond identifying the features of reflection to discovering how reflective teaching can be supported and encouraged. Questions that need to be asked include: How do teachers believe reflection contributes to teaching? What activities and conditions support reflection? How can they be achieved for the benefit of teaching and teacher learning? These overarching questions guided the research behind this book.

Researching these questions made it possible to understand the reality of reflection in the professional lives of experienced, practicing teachers and its relationship to teaching and learning. Current research offers little understanding of how reflection influences teachers' practice or the activities designed to enhance it (Richert, 1990). A primary goal of this research was to inquire into the role of reflection in teaching practice and the activities that encourage it. The results indicated that reflection, when supported by certain conditions, is indeed a powerful element of quality teaching.

Unfortunately, the daily realities of schools are not likely to foster reflection. The pace and structure of the school day, the implementation of multiple reforms, and a general lack of time have all been known to militate against reflective practice (Sarason, 1996). Thus proponents of reflection are faced with a challenge: how to encourage reflective activity in a setting that in many ways prevents it! In response to this contradictory and counterproductive situation, a secondary goal of the research was to develop an understanding of the conditions that influence reflection, with the hopes of determining which sustain and which obstruct reflective practice.

Overall, the information in this book responds to the new imperative to support and encourage reflective practice by bridging the gap between research that asserts its importance and a reality that threatens its existence.

THE BACKGROUND OF THE BOOK

To accomplish the goals described above, research behind this book examined the reflection of four high-school teachers recognized for the quality of their teaching. Input from the teachers on their reflective activities elicited descriptions and insights into reflection. The teachers' metareflections on these experiences—that is, their own thoughts about their experiences and the benefits of reflection—provided a detailed vision of what reflection is, how it contributes to teaching, and how it can be achieved.

Uniquely, this approach highlighted the perspectives of teachers recognized for their accomplishments, whose professional wisdom could enrich ideas about reflection in the field of education. These teachers were able to identify what research has typically overlooked: that some ways of reflecting have particular value to teaching and learning. Together, the activities they described formed a continuum, from wasteful exercises that did not promote reflection to reflective "aha" discoveries with the power to transform practice. Thus, it became evident that certain activities are likely to foster reflection, while others may shut it down.

The results of the research emphasized the features of reflection that mattered most in the experiences of four accomplished teachers, with implications for policy, practice, and professional development. Overall, the teachers' experiences and beliefs supported the idea that, despite a number of obstacles, reflection is a critical aspect of quality teaching—and one that should be valued as a professional activity of teaching.

A GUIDE TO SECTIONS AND CHAPTERS

The following sections and chapters describe and draw recommendations from the experiences of the four teachers mentioned above.

Section 1 explores the concept of reflection. A complex and multifaceted term, "reflection" connotes different ideas in different circumstances. Chapter 2 both describes the intricacies of reflection and connects them to the concept as a whole, forming a basis for discussion throughout the rest of the book. Chapter 3 provides more detailed information about the research informing the book. It explains the qualitative case study that took place and provides background for the examples used throughout the book to illustrate key points and substantiate recommendations.

Sections 2, 3, and 4 present, discuss, and contrast cases of reflection, or narrative descriptions of the teachers' experience. Cases highlight activities that illustrate both favorable and unfavorable circumstances for fostering reflection, allowing readers to learn from the mistakes and successes of real educators facing daily challenges and overcoming authentic obstacles. In section 2, chapters 4 through 10 focus on reflection in the daily life of teachers. In section 3, chapters 11 through 15 describe reflection in programs of professional development. In section 4, chapters 16 through 20 highlight how teachers reflected in ways of their personal choosing.

Finally, section 5 synthesizes the experiences of the four teachers with respect to reflection. Chapter 21 offers a practical summary of the advantages and disadvantages of different approaches to reflecting. The chapter identifies the characteristics of reflective activities that successfully promote teachers' professional growth and offers recommendations for educators who wish to promote quality teaching by supporting and encouraging reflective practice. Chapter 22 closes the book by affirming a significant belief held by the teachers featured in the book: that being thoughtful about teaching helps teachers to do their jobs well.

Before beginning an exploration of reflection in the next chapter, let us meet the four teachers whose experiences provide the cases of reflection used throughout the book.

PORTRAITS OF FOUR ACCOMPLISHED TEACHERS

The four teachers who participated in the research conducted for this book are all National Board certified teachers and recognized leaders in their schools and departments. These teachers consistently model exemplary reflective practice, making them rich sources for examples of reflection in teaching. It should be noted, however, that reflection underlies the practice of *all* teachers, not just the highly distinguished. Below, portraits of the teachers are presented to illustrate their personalities and practice—characteristics that undoubtedly shaped their experiences with reflection.

Kirk Underwood, High-School Science Teacher

Coach Underwood is a science teacher of eleven years at the high school he attended as a student. After graduating from college with a major in biology, he joined the faculty at Northern High School, where his former science teacher—a longtime member of the department—became a mentoring colleague. Underwood eventually earned his master's degree in science education and established a solid reputation as a science teacher, respected for his knowledge of the subject and his easy rapport with students. Quiet and understated, he approaches his classes with gentle intelligence—explaining complex theories and abstract concepts with simplicity, metaphors, and examples—then stirs things up with a boyish playfulness that captures the magic of science and sparks the attention of students. In this manner, he teaches Dalton's atomic theory by bouncing a red rubber ball, demonstrates mass ratio with fireballs and colorful flame, and paints purple signs with invisible chemicals that smolder secret messages to intrigued students.

Admittedly not a morning person, Underwood clutches a cup of coffee through most of his morning classes. His casual manner masks his steadfast energy, evidenced by his multiple roles. Coach of the swim team and adviser to the hiking club and the senior class, Underwood reveals himself to be a highly committed teacher respected by students and adults, inside and outside the classroom.

Ivy Green, High-School Mathematics Teacher

"How can you love math so much?" an amused student once asked Mrs. Green. A mathematics teacher with twelve years' experience, she wows students by "memorizing" the phone book using base-ten logic; she throws geometry surprise parties where students construct pi by measuring pumpkins; she uses literature to illustrate mathematical concepts, such as when she uses "Zeno's Paradoxes" (e.g., Hofstadter, 1979) to explain infinite limits and Edwin Abbot's *Flatland* (1953) to enrich understanding of geometry. Just from listening to Ivy Green talk, it is obvious she *does* love math that much.

She understands it, too, and communicates that understanding to students. By simplifying concepts for students and linking ideas together to help them construct understanding, she makes the course content she teaches at Southern High School—algebra, geometry, trigonometry, and calculus—accessible to students.

Outside the classroom, Green is a model and a mentor for teachers. An annual participant in the regional math conference, a cooperating teacher for preservice teachers, a leading member of her department, and a facilitator for National Board certification candidates, she is active in her profession. Her involvement in these various activities keeps her current and helps her contribute to the field. Still, she maintains balance in her life by leaving plenty of time to play with her preschool-aged daughter before school and joining her family for get-togethers on weekends. With creativity and insight, she teaches math in a way that keeps her excited about her profession and effective with students.

Mary King, High-School History and Social Studies Teacher

Mrs. King, with a new name after her recent marriage and with thirty years of teaching under her belt, is a leader at the history department of Eastern High School. Her experience and wisdom create an easy assurance that comes from a deep knowledge of her subject and the talent to share it with students. Her list of credentials is long. Now teaching

American government, in former years she has taught U.S. history, world history, culture and religion, and an integrated history/English block. At Eastern, she has been the department chair and a regular member of pilot teams and design committees for new projects. She is known for her role as a leader in the district; her accomplishments there include roles in professional development, new teacher mentoring, and assessment.

In her classroom, King is comfortable and keen. Standing in a cluster of listening seniors, with one hand in her pocket and the other gesturing as she makes a point, she asks the hard questions about life in a democracy and pushes students to think about their political stances. Passionate about civic duty and democratic responsibility, she generously reaches into her deep stores of knowledge about history and politics and offers rich information to students, helping them see beyond the brevity of their eighteen-year experience and understand how the American past has led to politics in the twenty-first century.

Laura Nichols, High-School English Teacher

Energetic and bold, Mrs. Nichols is the Western High School teacher about whom students say with admiration, "Her class is *hard!*" With thirty-one years of experience, she is acclaimed for her excellence in teaching by her colleagues, who awarded her the honor of state teacher of the year and celebrated in her classroom, where a bulletin board overflows with photographs of students who love her. Her involvement in every aspect of educational life is impressive and diverse. They include areas related to her subject matter (like department chair and head of the AP program), teacher education (as a cooperating teacher, mentor, and college instructor), professional development (as a regular participant in a small professional group), and student life (as a ski club adviser).

At home in her classroom and surrounded by students, she is the consummate teacher at every moment of the day. She masterfully engages students about mythology one moment and teaches them life skills the next; she takes time out of English class to help students reflect on their progress-report grades and stays late to read and respond to their college essays. Even with the experience gained from an illustrious career, Nichols approaches her days with a manner at once confident and humble, serious and fun loving. On any given day, she can be heard asking students what *she* can do better so *they* will succeed, and closing conversations with an "I love you!" and a motherly squeeze.

Model Teachers, Typical Schools

All four of these teachers are acknowledged by their colleagues for the quality of their teaching and their professional contributions. They have also each earned the highest distinction currently available for educators: certification by the National Board for Professional Teaching Standards. In all cases, these teachers represent exemplary practice. Their experiences introduce rich contexts for the study of reflection; their practice presents "images of the possible" (Shulman, 1987) and illustrates the role of reflection in quality teaching. As such, they also hint at the potential for all teachers to teach effectively and reflectively when the right conditions, like professional support and opportunities for ongoing learning, are present.

As white teachers in moderately wealthy districts, they are privileged to enjoy many of those conditions. Their school contexts offer the opportunity and support necessary to succeed within and outside the walls of their classrooms. But even in fortunate circumstances, the conditions are far from ideal. The schools in which these teachers teach are large, typical high schools, where time is short and money is tight. Examining the experiences of accomplished teachers under the constraints of the public-school environment offers a chance to gain insight into the realities of teaching, which have implications for reflective practice in American schools. Given the disparity between schools with differing racial and economic profiles, it is fair to surmise that struggles are exacerbated and advantages fewer for educators in less-fortunate circumstances. It is with reality fully in mind that we should view these four teachers' experiences as an illustration of the role of reflection in teachers' practice.

SUMMARY

This chapter has discussed the importance of reflection in quality teaching—an aspect of teaching emphasized in research but harder to achieve in practice. Three key questions will be explored throughout the book: How do teachers believe reflection contributes to teaching? What activities and conditions support reflection? How can these activities and conditions be achieved for the benefit of teaching and learning? This book will examine these questions as it considers cases from four accomplished teachers' practice. First, however, the next chapter will discuss the concept of reflection in depth, laying a foundation for the cases of reflection in teaching.

Chapter Two

Reflection in Teaching: Reviewing the Research

What is reflection? Its derivation is the Latin *reflectere,* meaning "to bend back." It has applications in grammar, physics, and psychology. Grammatically, a pronoun is reflexive if it used as an object to refer to the subject of a verb, as in "I prepared *myself* for the journey." In physics, reflection is the return of light, heat, or sound after striking a surface. In psychological terms, reflection refers to a mental image or representation. The original Latin meaning of "bending back" is apparent in each of these cases.

—L. Valli, Listening to Other Voices

What is reflection in teaching? Before exploring teachers' reflective practice, it will help to clarify our terms. A complex and multifaceted term, "reflection" connotes different meanings in different circumstances. This chapter summarizes various aspects of reflection so as to better understand its role in teaching and teacher learning. Elements of this chapter include a definition of reflection, a description of reflection in teaching, a list of activities known to support reflection, and a discussion of the benefits of reflection, as well as the threats to its survival in schools and the professional lives of teachers.

A DEFINITION OF REFLECTION

What is reflection, exactly? Perhaps the best-known theorist on the topic is Dewey (1910, p. 6), who writes that reflective thought "is the active, persistent, and careful consideration of any belief or supposed form of

11

knowledge in the light of the grounds that support it and the further conclusions to which it tends" (p. 6). Elaborating, he describes such thought as conscious and voluntary, based on evidence and rationality, and supported by a disposition of open-mindedness, wholeheartedness, and responsibility.

Although Dewey proposed these ideas nearly a century ago, the spirit of the concept remains the same. Yet, we know far more now about reflection and its connection to teaching. Researchers and educators alike have contributed to the development of a more detailed definition of reflection that is useful for understanding its role in teaching. Key ideas from this body of knowledge are described below.

Reflection on, in, and for Action

Donald Schön (1983), who studied professionals at work to understand the role of reflection, describes it as a process in which a person tries to deal with and make sense of "some puzzling or troubling or interesting phenomenon" while simultaneously reflecting on "the understandings which have been implicit in his action, understandings which he surfaces, criticizes, restructures, and embodies in further action" (Schön, 1983, p. 50). In short, reflection involves shuttling back and forth between thinking and action. However, the process may appear differently in different situations. One useful way to understand this complexity is to consider when it takes place. Three categories break down the concept more specifically: reflection-on-action, reflection-in-action, and reflection-for-action.

Reflection-on-Action

Perhaps the most familiar image of reflection involves a sequence of *action* then *thought*. Reflection in this case means pausing after an activity to see how it went—to ask what went well, what didn't, and what could be changed for the next time. Schön (1983; 1987) discovered that professionals would indeed look back on their practice after completing a task. He called this *reflection-on-action*. In teaching, such reflection may take place at the end of a school day or even at the end of the year.

Reflection-in-Action

Other ways of reflecting are equally important. Schön (1983; 1987) found that, at times, professionals would actually reflect in the very midst of work. He called this *reflection-in-action,* a process involving thought *during* action.

Likening the process to jazz improvisation, Schön (1983) describes reflection-in-action as the interweaving of thinking and action that allows people to deal well with uncertain, unstable, unique, and value-laden situations. For instance, teachers may improvise, or reflect-in-action, when they suddenly realize they are losing the attention of their students. Similarly, reflection-in-action may involve puzzling problems and attempts to make sense of them—for example, when a teachers tries to figure out why a student isn't grasping a concept and then tries new ways to aid understanding. In these instances, reflection takes place in the midst of action, not after the fact.

Reflection-for-Action

Expanding on Schön's ideas (1983) about reflection-on-action and reflection-in-action, Killion and Todnem (1991) propose one more way that reflection takes place: *reflection-for-action.* The process involves *thought* then *action.* With this idea, they assert that reflection is a practical tool for guiding future practice, that it is

> the desired outcome of both previous types of reflection. We undertake reflection, not so much to revisit the past or to become aware of the metacognitive process one is experiencing (both noble reasons in themselves), but to guide future action (the more practical purpose). (p. 15)

Killion and Todnem suggest that all three types of reflection—before, after, and for the sake of future action—are important elements of practice.

The Cycle of Reflection

While useful for understanding reflection, the idea of reflecting in, on, and for action can be somewhat misleading, for it disconnects what is actually a fluid, iterative process. Combining these ideas presents a more accurate picture of the activities of teaching that, together, constitute a cycle of reflection.

For example, Grossman and Shulman (1994) describe the reflection on, in, and for action as being akin to the processes of pedagogical reasoning. They propose that teachers reflect *for* action as they engage in curriculum analysis and planning, that they reflect *in* action during active instruction, and that they reflect *on* both action and thought as they review and evaluate their practice. This contributes to a better understanding of the sequence of reflection as it takes place in the context of teaching. Importantly, the correlation between reflection and pedagogical reasoning also suggests that, in the various activities of teaching, all three types of reflection take place and, correspondingly, that reflection is inherent in all of the intellectual processes of teaching.

One More Definition

To capture the complete cycle of reflection in a more condensed form, we can rely on a summative definition:

Reflection is looking back on experience in a way that informs practice, learning in the midst of practice, and/or making informed and intelligent decisions about what to do, when to do it, and why it should be done. (Shulman, 1987; Richert, 1990; Schön, 1983)

This definition is sufficiently broad to capture the various ways teachers reflect. This definition will be used throughout the book to explore all kinds of reflection in teaching.

However, understanding such a complex process requires more than a broad definition. Specifically, three areas of interest will inform the discussion: (1) varieties of reflection in teaching, (2) reflective activities in the context of teaching, and (3) teachers' perspectives of reflection.

VARIETIES OF REFLECTION IN TEACHING

Reading about reflection, one finds a seemingly endless variety of forms. This book reveals a number of these in the cases of teachers' experiences.

Here, an overview of the varieties is provided as context for the cases. This section discusses different types of reflection that surface and how these types may vary in quality. Understanding these nuances in reflection sheds light on the way reflection looks and sounds in the daily lives of teachers.

TYPES OF REFLECTION

Because reflection is so complex and its varieties so numerous and unique, researchers have identified categories of reflection to describe how it looks in real life.

For example, Van Manen (1977) describes "levels of reflectivity." At the lower levels, reflection involves technical application of knowledge and skills in the classroom setting. Midlevel reflection emphasizes examination of the assumptions underlying practice. The highest level emphasizes moral and ethical issues that directly and indirectly impact the classroom, such as justice and equity. The levels include increasingly "higher" forms of thought, moving from issues of practicality to values and beliefs.

Similarly, Valli (1997) identifies five types of reflection that she views as hierarchical. In her model, "technical" reflection involves comparing one's teaching practice to external guidelines, such as those for research and standards. "Reflection in/on action" involves making decisions about teaching in unique classroom situations. "Deliberative" reflection involves weighing viewpoints and research to understand various concerns of teaching. "Personalistic" reflection is focused on personal growth and relationships; it involves listening to one's own inner voice, as well as to others, to gain perspective on a given situation. Finally, "critical" reflection is concerned with social, moral, and political issues and involves judging the ultimate purposes of schooling. In her explanation of these types, Valli suggests that they form a hierarchy. For example, teachers may first need to reflect on areas of technical knowledge and skill (technical reflection) before being facile in comparing different teaching strategies (deliberative reflection). She notes that each type has strengths and limitations and that each holds value for teachers. However, she also implies that some types of reflection take on a certain moral importance, arguing in particular that critical reflection, with its emphasis on justice and democracy, is "ultimately more important" than others (p. 82).

A third useful categorization of the different types of reflection is provided by Zeichner (1994). This framework ties different types of reflection to traditions in educational reform, emphasizing that each of the types derives from different underlying assumptions about the aims of education. He defines the categories as follows:

Academic: emphasizes disciplinary knowledge;

Social Efficiency: emphasizes "generic" knowledge and skills in teaching; includes knowledge base, skills orientation, deliberation, flexibility, and judgment;

Developmentalist: emphasizes the development of the student and the teacher; includes teacher as naturalist, teacher as researcher, and teacher as artist;

Social Reconstructivist: emphasizes social justice and equity, as well as care and compassion; includes inward and outward reflection;

Generic: emphasizes reflective practice in general as central to teaching and teacher education, without a particular focus on the content, quality, or context of reflection.

Throughout his presentation of these five traditions, Zeichner points out that none of them are distinct or mutually exclusive. Each of the traditions incorporates components of the others; the difference is a matter of emphasis.

The categories described by Van Manen (1977), Valli (1997), and Zeichner (1994) provide just a sample of the ways in which researchers have noted different types of reflection in teaching. Other researchers have proposed similar—and different—ideas. However, these three models are sufficient for making the point that the term "reflection" can connote many different meanings.

Understanding the differences between types of reflection is valuable for understanding and promoting reflective practice. Taking an academic or technical approach to reflection, for example, will yield a different understanding of teaching than will a critical approach. Both are important, and, yet, they are very distinct. Distinguishing between types of reflection, therefore, can help teachers become more deliberate and well rounded in their approach.

The purpose of this book, however, is not simply to classify cases of reflective practice. Rather, it is to examine those cases to understand whether and how all types of reflection can be supported. Although these categories provide useful background information to prepare us to understand the various ways teachers reflect on their practice, they do little to provide tools for analysis needed to view cases of experience for the purposes of learning how best to promote reflection. Three central questions proposed by Grimmett et al. (1990) are therefore useful in analyzing—not to mention designing—instances of reflective practice. These are:

1. What is being reflected upon?
2. How is the reflective process engaged?
3. What is the purpose of the reflection? (p. 36)

These questions apply across varieties of reflection and can be useful for understanding what values a given type of reflection embodies and the ultimate purpose it serves.

Notably, the experiences of the teachers featured in this book revealed an important limitation to studying varieties of reflection in teaching. While different types of reflection served different purposes with different results, the *value* of the experiences also varied. Some of the teachers' experiences with reflection seemed somehow more substantial or meaningful than others—a question about the quality of reflection.

THE QUALITY OF REFLECTION

As important as the varieties of reflection, the quality of reflection also impacts the usefulness of reflection to teachers. In their reflective activities, teachers must move from surface-level descriptions of practice to significant advances in learning and growth. In fostering reflection among teachers, questions of quality are particularly significant in terms of the practical application of the results. To promote reflection without a sound understanding of how quality can vary is to risk perpetuating reflective activities with no clear sense of which of those activities are most effective or why. Just as quality teaching enhances student learning, quality reflection enhances quality teaching.

How can one identify the quality of reflection? Identifying layers of quality reflection can help teachers not just to identify reflection, but to lead themselves from superficial to significant reflection (Jay & Johnson, 2002;

Hess, 1999; McKenna, 1999). For instance, Jay and Johnson (2002) describe a progression from "descriptive" to "comparative" to "critical" reflection. The National Board for Professional Teaching Standards (2001) calls for "descriptive," "analytic," and "reflective" thought to prompt teachers' writing about practice. Even the concept of "lower order" versus "higher order" thinking skills, familiar from Bloom's taxonomy (1956), can be helpful in studying differences in the quality of reflection. Each of these attempts to distinguish between the qualities of different kinds of thinking can be instructive for exploring the quality of different kinds of reflection. Together, they suggest that reflection is more valuable when it moves from surface levels to more substantial, more grounded, more sophisticated levels of thinking.

Whereas varieties of reflection are interesting to consider when examining teachers' reflective activities, the quality of reflection is absolutely essential. As seen in the cases presented later in the book, the teachers reported that some experiences with reflection were trivial and others were profound, with significant effects on their teaching. We will discover that the activities themselves actually influence the effectiveness of reflection—the next subject covered here.

REFLECTIVE ACTIVITIES AND
THE CONTEXTS OF TEACHING

Teachers know that reflection can occur anytime, anywhere. But reflection can also be encouraged directly by structuring activities to support it in the various contexts of teachers' professional lives. Whether in the classroom, at a university, or in the staff room, among countless other possibilities, teachers may engage in reflection. And yet, these contexts differ in diverse and fundamental ways that influence the type and quality of reflection. Considering the conditions that support reflection is vital. Fortunately, researchers have provided valuable information about which activities foster reflection.

Reflective Activities

How are various kinds of reflection enacted and encouraged in teaching? How do different activities construct the content, process, and purpose of reflection? And what do they contribute to practice? Researchers have advanced thinking on teachers' reflection by asking such questions and studying the processes and products of reflective activities. Their findings raise three important points.

First, researchers have found that certain activities promote reflection *differently* than others. Common activities include journal writing (journaling), portfolio creation, conversations with colleagues, evaluations of practice, reflective interviews, peer observation, group seminars, videotapes of practice, analysis of practice according to standards, and analysis of student work. One study (Richert, 1990) revealed that specific characteristics of various activities contributed to teachers' reflection, suggesting that the nature of an activity shaped the form of reflection. For example, watching videotape of their own teaching may provoke teachers to analyze instructional style, whereas analyzing student work might lead them to understand students' misconceptions of content. This showed that structured opportunities to reflect, along with necessary resources and support, were imperative for teachers to be reflective.

Second, researchers have found that certain activities promote reflection *more effectively* than others. Collier (1999) found that many structured activities encouraged only the most basic types of reflection. Few pushed teachers to examine assumptions and see teaching from a new perspective. Collier supports the development of proactive habits that help teachers expand their ideas so they can move beyond questions of "what went well and what didn't" to asking "whose interests does my teaching serve, and whose does it not?"—the kind of question that leads to the deepest, most critical levels of reflection.

Third, researchers have found certain activities promote reflection *more systematically* than others. They assert that quality reflection depends on well-structured activity. As studied by Wildman et al. (1990), carefully designed activities (such as discussion groups or portfolio creation) fostered a more systematic approach to reflection than naturally occurred, suggesting that such activities could be an important tool in teachers' learning and growth. However, the researchers also asserted that "schools are difficult environments for reflective thinking" (p. 160), raising questions about how and when such activities could actually take place.

If structured activities for reflection are crucial to its effectiveness, but the school environment itself makes reflection difficult, how do teachers reflect on their practice? This raises two contradictory themes, discussed below: first, that any teaching-related context can incorporate reflection and, second, that almost no such context is ideal. This dilemma warrants discussion about the contexts of reflection and the conditions of teaching.

The Contexts of Reflection

On one level, almost any context can be appropriate for reflection. Darling-Hammond and McLaughlin (1995) suggest that common tasks of teaching all have the potential to provide learning experiences. Some of these include such *ordinary events* as department meetings, mentoring programs, and committee work. Some of these include *supplementary professional activities,* like peer review and study groups. Some of these even include *professional involvement outside of school,* like school/university partnerships, teacher-to-teacher networks, and involvement at district, regional, and national levels. In other words, virtually any context in which teachers work has potential to provide opportunities for reflection. Unfortunately, this potential isn't likely to be realized when one considers the common conditions of teaching and schools.

Despite the plausible potential for any teaching-related context to provide opportunities for reflection, research on the contexts of teacher learning implies that they are not conducive to reflection in reality. The works of Sarason (1990; 1996) and Fullan and Miles (1992) provide some of the most thorough and striking arguments as to why the structures of schools are likely to constrain opportunities for reflection. These authors describe the typical structure of schools as built on a bureaucratic "factory model" that controls time and activity. They argue that top-down models for administrative decision making accentuate the power structure and introduce political issues that can have a number of constraining effects on the conditions within the school contexts, including ineffective communication, work overload, isolation, and feelings of powerlessness. Even efforts at change that come from outside the school (e.g., from consultants and new programs) can be threatened by conditions within the school, because they don't address the organizational structure; instead they are added to a system already under stress (Sarason, 1996). These characteristics don't bode well for the potential of school contexts to nurture opportunities for reflection, which are often believed to require time, trust, and communication.

The probable tendency for organizational issues to provide obstacles to reflection is compounded by the culture of schools. Palmer (1998) describes a climate of competition and isolation that exists among teachers—a culture that can divide teachers even though collaboration might seem more beneficial.

> Resources that could help us teach better are available from each other—if we could get access to them. But there, of course, is the rub. Academic culture builds barriers between colleagues even higher and wider than those between us and our students. These barriers come partly from the competition that keeps us fragmented by fear. But they also come from the fact that teaching is perhaps the most privatized of all the public professions. (p. 142)

In such a culture, collaboration among colleagues—again, a condition beneficial to reflective activity—is not likely to occur.

Despite these issues of school structure and culture, some teachers certainly do manage to reflect on their practice. But given the constraints on reflection, one wonders how it fares in the real lives of teachers. This book illustrates the ways in which reflection has or has not been encouraged and enacted by the arrangement of different activities for four specific teachers. Under what conditions does reflection thrive and under what conditions does it falter? This question can help us understand how practicing teachers actually experience reflection. But one more critical piece is missing that is necessary for getting the full picture of their experience: the perspectives of the teachers themselves.

TEACHERS' PERSPECTIVES ON REFLECTION

This chapter has discussed varieties of reflection and activities that support it—two ways of understanding what reflection is and what it contributes to teaching. But we can also learn much about reflection by getting the perspectives of teachers on their own experiences with reflection. In this book, the opinions of teachers are highly valued, under the assumption that teachers' expertise may be the best lens into reflection and in the belief that much can be learned from their "wisdom of practice" (Shulman, 1987).

The Wisdom of Practice

As professionals, teachers carry with them a vast store of experience. The resulting wisdom takes into account their expertise and validates its importance. In Shulman's words, "It is the wisdom of practice itself that guides (or provide rationalizations for) the practices of able teachers" (Shulman, 1987, p. 11)—suggesting that quality teachers are a key resource for understanding quality teaching.

In this book, the teachers who shared their experiences with reflection were all considered to be leaders in their schools, experts in their field, and highly accomplished teachers. Learning from them and tapping into their "wisdom of practice," we can uncover the activities in which they have engaged, why they perceived these activities to be valuable, and these activities' relationship to reflection. The words of these teachers can help us understand how their reflective experiences grew out of and informed the practice of teaching.

The Value of Teachers' Perspectives

The focus on teachers' own perspectives on their experiences is less common in research than one might think. In most of the literature on teachers' reflection, the teachers' perspective is deemphasized. Even research studies of reflection in which teachers are participants focus only superficially on teachers' own thinking about the role of reflection in their work, highlighting their *reflection* (e.g., Collier, 1999), but not their *thinking about reflection*. However, this kind of metareflection (Richert, 1990) is critical to understanding the role of reflection in teaching and attempts to foster its occurrence. Therefore, in this book, the teachers' perspective is central in identifying the quality of reflection, allowing us to discover how experienced teachers perceive the potentially reflective activities in which they participate, as valuable, trivial, or something in between. Moreover, the invitation to teachers to comment on their experience openly allowed them to reveal their emotions and their motivations for participating in a range of activities, both reflective and nonreflective, that can be instructive for creating and supporting reflective activities for teachers.

SUMMARY

This chapter has identified a definition of reflection. It has discussed the many varieties of reflection, which may differ in both type and quality. We have seen that reflection depends in large part on the activities in which it takes place, and we have learned that teachers' perspectives lend credence and insight to the value of reflection in their work. This overview of reflection lays the groundwork for understanding and promoting reflection in the daily lives of teachers.

It also laid the groundwork for the research behind this book. Interested readers will find a description of this research in the next chapter, which discusses the qualitative case study on which the book is based. This chapter may be skipped by readers wishing to move directly into the cases of the teachers' experience, which begin in chapter 4.

Chapter Three

A Qualitative Case Study of Reflection: Research Methods

"How can we draw valid meaning from [research]? What . . . will get us knowledge that we and others can rely on?" (Miles & Huberman, 1994, p. 1). These questions concern researchers and readers alike. This chapter discusses the research behind this book.

The contents of the book came from a study designed to build understanding of reflection in the practical realities of teachers. Importantly, it relied on teachers' expertise and experience—or "wisdom of practice" (Shulman, 1987)—to inform ideas about reflection and attempts to foster it in teaching. To describe the research process, this chapter is divided into three parts. The first overviews the study and the research questions. The second breaks down the concept of reflection into key categories for analyzing teachers' experience. The third briefly explains the research process. Together, these sections provide a sense of how the cases and conclusions of the book were derived.

AN OVERVIEW OF THE STUDY AND RESEARCH QUESTIONS

In the study, four accomplished teachers were observed and interviewed with respect to their experiences with reflection. Five research questions guided this study.

1. How do experienced teachers think about the notion of reflection?
2. In what different ways do teachers reflect on, in, and for their practice?

3. How do the content, process, and goals of reflection vary in different activities?
4. What benefits and limitations do teachers associate with reflection? What personal and professional gains do they realize? What are the gains for student learning?
5. What conditions nurture or constrain reflective practice for these teachers?

These questions were used to examine teachers' reflection in the different contexts of their professional lives and to learn about the role of reflection in their teaching.

Arising from a qualitative case study, the results are not claimed to generalize to all teachers in all circumstances. Rather, the experiences of these four teachers provide insight into some of the challenges and benefits of reflection in the life of a teacher.

KEY CONCEPTS IN STUDYING REFLECTION

As noted earlier, reflection is complex and multifaceted. Researching teachers' reflection required breaking down the concepts even further, so as to analyze the teachers' experiences in detail. These concepts, or "dimensions," are described below.

Dimensions of Reflection

Three key dimensions were useful in comparing different instances of reflection: content, process, and goals (Grimmett et al., 1990).

Content. The content of reflection is the matter upon which a teacher reflects. Topics are limitless, but may include curriculum (e.g., what to teach), pedagogy (e.g., instructional strategies), students (e.g., development and understanding), equity (e.g., race and gender issues), and the profession (values and beliefs about teaching and the self).

Process. Several processes take place in reflection. The cycle often starts with a "puzzle of practice" (Munby & Russell, 1990)—some intriguing or troublesome matter. Reflecting on that "puzzle" typically includes description, comparison, analysis, judgment, and renewed understanding (Dewey,

1933; Grimmett et al., 1990; Hess, 1999; Schön, 1983). Clearly, reflection is not a single event, but a process.

Goal/Purpose. The goals of reflection can vary (Wolf, 1994). A teacher reflecting on a student's struggle hopes to improve that student's learning, whereas a teacher reflecting on curriculum may want to enhance student engagement. Often, reflection meets more than one goal.

Dimensions of Activities

Activities commonly thought to be reflective include journaling, critiquing instruction, analyzing student work, creating portfolios, and studying videotaped teaching, to name a few. Each has different characteristics and results (Richert, 1990). Such activities may be broken down further to understand how they support reflection. For example, the content, process, and goals of reflection are likely to differ according to the elements of the activity. One teacher may reflect on a failed lesson (content) by journaling (process) in order to improve it (goal), while another may reflect on the socioeconomic status of her students (content) by holding a discussion forum (process) in order to close the achievement gap (goal). The activities undertaken by these two teachers would differ markedly, yet both count as reflection.

Additionally, features of the activities may have an impact on reflection by directing teachers' attention in a particular way or giving them a unique perspective from which to reflect. Most importantly, activities differ as to whether they occurred naturally or were facilitated by an external source. Other differentiating features include the other people involved (e.g., students, colleagues, facilitators, administrators), the medium (e.g., thought, writing, dialogue, videotape), materials used to frame the activity (e.g., directions, guidelines, questions, standards), and the degree to which reflection occurs naturally or is facilitated by some external source. Each may cause a teacher to experience reflection differently.

Dimensions of reflection and reflective activities are useful for understanding the characteristics of reflection in a variety of circumstances. But they offer little help in appreciating the conditions in which reflection is either nurtured or constrained or understanding how and when reflection contributes to teachers' practice. For this, we must examine dimensions of the contexts within which it takes place.

Dimensions of Context

A wide range of conditions may influence reflective experience (Jay, 2001). Issues of structure, culture, time, money, encouragement, support, motivation, and capacity are all important to consider in studying teachers' experiences with reflection, and they are ever present in schools and classrooms in which reflection is likely to occur.

Although possible contexts for reflection are limitless, certain contexts were expected to hold particular potential as contexts for reflective activities:

- Meetings, classrooms, and other school-based contexts.
- Contexts of assessment and evaluation inside and outside of schools.
- Mentoring relationships, collegial relationships, and teachers' friendships.
- Programs for teacher learning, professional development, and school change.

These contexts were of particular interest among the teachers' experiences.

Dimensions of Teachers' Perspectives

Reflective activities can be analyzed not just for the way they are designed or might be expected to occur, but for how they occur in the minds of the participating teachers. This study provided the opportunity to inquire directly into what teachers think and how they feel about participating in various activities, which has bearing on whether and when teachers are likely to reflect, as well as how reflection can be enhanced or encouraged.

As part of the study, the teachers were asked about the gains they believed resulted from reflection. Such gains could be personal, teaching related, or student related. All of these constitute legitimate outcomes of teacher reflection. Understanding their relationship to particular activities is useful for understanding the effects of reflective activities and designing activities with a specific purpose in mind.

To review, this study explored the relationship between the content, process, and goals/purposes of reflection and the activities within which reflection takes place. A variety of reflective activities exist that may occur naturally or be facilitated and that contain features that can be compared, such as people, medium, and materials. The effectiveness of activities may be impacted by the presence or absence of contextual factors that nurture or constrain reflectivity. Teachers' perspectives of the activity and the gains they believe they receive may also influence the success, or quality, of the reflective experience. Having described in broad terms the study, research questions, and key concepts in studying reflection, the discussion now turns to the methods used in the research.

RESEARCH METHODS

The study employed a qualitative approach in examining reflection in the reflective activities of a small number of teachers in the contexts of their practice. This section describes sampling strategies, data sources, and analysis techniques of the study.

Choosing Study Participants

As a rule, qualitative studies are small, purposeful, and theory driven (Miles & Huberman, 1994). For this reason, only four teachers were chosen to participate in the study. The choice of teachers depended on three factors: individual characteristics, the settings in which they taught, and their affiliation with the National Board for Professional Teaching Standards (NBPTS). All of these were expected to generate a rich set of data providing multiple opportunities to witness reflection. These three factors in selection are discussed in more detail below.

Participants

Participants for this study were four experienced teachers with a variety of experiences with reflection who were all able to clearly articulate their thinking processes and describe their experiences. A small number of participants made it possible to study reflective experiences in detail and in depth—an essential goal of the study. For the sake of contrast, it was important to select participants who had shared experiences. To achieve this, participants were selected who had created portfolios for the National Board for Professional Teaching Standards—a process that involved completing several activities generally thought to be reflective (Richert, 1990). Although this approach couldn't ensure that participants would be characteristically reflective, it did provide an opportunity to talk to teachers who had experienced a variety of reflective processes.

The participants were high-school teachers representing a range of subject areas—English, social studies, mathematics, and science—the core academic disciplines of the secondary curriculum. The teachers included both women (three) and men (one), to allow contrast of potential gender-related preferences for certain kinds of thought (Carter, 1993; Clandinin, 1986; Noddings, 1986). Participants ranged in years of experience from approximately ten to more than thirty years—a range expected to highlight the tendency for teachers to become more reflective and reflect more instinctively as they gain experience (Wildman et al., 1990). Choosing participants with a mixture of traits in this way created a well-rounded opportunity to study reflection in a variety of ways.

Settings

As noted above, reflection can occur in both naturally occurring and facilitated activities. Both were studied in the research process.

Naturally occurring activities were likely to happen in the course of teachers' everyday practice. Thus, teachers were observed and queried in the course of their practice. Instances of reflection and the factors that enhanced or constrained reflective practice were expected to be found in a variety of settings, including the classrooms, halls, and meeting spaces where the teachers spent their working days.

Facilitated activities were expected to occur within specifically designed programs. Studying teachers' reflection in facilitated activities involved interviewing teachers about their experiences with the activities involved in creating an NBPTS portfolio that had potential to promote reflectivity, as well as an analysis of the portfolios themselves. These activities included writing about practice, applying and discussing the use of standards in the context of teaching, analyzing student work, and observing oneself on videotape. The teachers were involved in other programs besides the National Board, such as critical friends groups and mentoring programs.

Teachers were therefore observed and interviewed with regard to those experiences, as well.

Having chosen study participants based on their characteristics, the settings in which their reflection was likely to take place, and the their affiliation with the National Board, the study proceeded by searching for data from a number of sources.

Data Sources

Data for the study were drawn from a series of interviews, observations, and documents expected to shed light on the teachers' reflection.

Interviews

The interviews conducted as the foundational source of data were semi-structured clinical interviews (Ginsburg, 1981; Patton, 1980), the use of which helped prepare questions to guide but not constrain the direction of interviews. This technique made it possible to ask consistent questions of all the teachers, while maintaining flexibility for understanding their unique experiences. In the interviews, the teachers described experiences with reflection, explained their reflective activities, and discussed conditions that influenced or could be designed to enhance their ability to be reflective.

These interviews were the primary source of data. Other strategies used included observations, documents, and additional data sources, as discussed below.

Observations

Teachers were observed in their practice to complement, provide material for, and extend information gathered in interviews. To do this involves

> participating, overtly or covertly, in people's daily lives for an extended period of time, watching what happens, listening to what is said, asking questions—in fact, collecting whatever data are available to throw light on the issues that are the focus of the research. (Hammersley & Atkinson, 1995, p. 1)

This approach was beneficial for studying reflection in teachers' practice and for discovering consistencies or inconsistencies between what the teachers said in their interviews and what was observed in their practice. Contexts for observations included:

Classroom settings: in which teaching often evolved from one class to the next and day to day (a process often stemming from reflection in action);

School settings: in which teachers talked with colleagues, potentially reflecting on and for practice, that is, before school, at lunch, after school, and during meetings;

Professional development settings: in which it became possible to observe structures in place that might involve reflection on and for practice, such as study groups, critical friends groups, mentoring situations, and casual conversations.

These contexts were systematically observed so as to include different days of the week, different times of day, and a variety of whole-school, small-group, and individual experiences with both naturally occurring and facilitated activities for reflection.

Observing in the contexts of teachers' practice made it possible to note other elements of teachers' professional experiences that influenced reflection—for example, the structure and pace of the school day, arrangements that helped or limited teachers' abilities to be reflective, and the culture and climate of different settings and interactions.

Documents and Additional Data Sources

A variety of other data sources were used to get a diverse perspective on teachers' experiences. Evidence took many forms: materials from programs in which the teachers were involved (such as portfolio directions, guidelines, and prompts), information about structured activities and the organizations that designed them (from websites and published information), lesson plans, handouts, student work, and journal entries. These sources were helpful in providing detail about the nature of reflective activities, their influences on teaching, and the conditions of context affecting the teachers' reflection.

Conversational Interviews

Throughout the data-gathering process, teachers continually answered questions and provided insights in conversational interviews (Patton,

1980). These provided a way for teachers to describe information that may not have been visible or apparent to an observer (i.e., teachers' thoughts, insights, and silent unobservable reflection).

Stimulated Recall Tasks

A stimulated recall process was used to explore experiences with activities that could not be directly observed. Such tasks were used to explore teachers' reflection in the context of their NBPTS portfolios. These involved asking teachers to review sections of their portfolios, then (using those sections as prompts) to recall their experiences. A similar technique was used to have teachers reflect on observed practice. They read summaries of observation notes, then responded by "thinking aloud" (Ericsson & Simon, 1980; Pressley & Afflerbach, 1995)—a technique inviting them to clarify and discuss the role of reflection in observed activities.

Data Analysis

Analyzing the data involved a process of induction, deduction, and verification common to a grounded theory approach (Strauss, 1987). The process is described below.

Data preparation. Following interviews and observations, transcripts and summaries were prepared and made available to teachers for clarification and verification. Transcripts were coded using qualitative analysis techniques (Huberman & Miles, 1992), which revealed distinct instances of reflection. The next phase of analysis focused exclusively on these instances.

Identification of reflective instances. This phase of analysis involved the selection and examination of instances of reflection described by the teachers. "Instances" were defined as teachers' storied examples of reflection in, on, and for practice. The teachers also included stories of *missed* opportunities for reflection, which provided an important contrast in the research.

Analysis and case study of reflection. Each of the individual cases of reflection and nonreflection were analyzed, compared, and contrasted in order to gain insight into the teachers' experiences. Particularly salient were (1) the different types of activities represented in the instances (e.g., participating in small groups, creating portfolio entries), (2) the different conditions within which the activities took place (i.e., contextual factors such as time, place, and climate), and (3) the teachers' perceptions of the value of the reflection (e.g., as not valuable, valuable, or very valuable). Instances were labeled, sorted, and classified for comparison and examination. Ultimately, three overarching contexts emerged:

1. inside the school (meetings and individual or group activities),
2. outside the school (programs of teacher assessment),
3. outside the school (self-selected, self-initiated activities).

Readers will recognize these contexts as being the three overarching contexts into which the cases of reflection are grouped in this book. In the most detailed phase of analysis, instances within each context were analyzed one more time to search for patterns among reflective experiences within those contexts—including such elements as the content of reflection, the process, the goals and purpose, the people involved, the materials used, the medium (e.g., written, spoken), the benefits and limitations of reflection within the experience, the contextual factors, and the teachers' perceptions of the experience. Subsequently, comparisons were made by using data displays, which map ideas into a single, visual space (Miles & Huberman, 1994) and make emerging propositions apparent as patterns become evident (Erickson, 1985).

Five propositions eventually emerged from the data. First, whether reflective opportunities are available for teachers may vary according to the overarching context in which teachers' reflection takes place. Second, reflective and nonreflective activities may be meaningful or not. Third, teachers may initiate reflective activities for themselves when opportunities do not otherwise exist. Fourth, reflective experiences range in their perceived value by teachers from not at all valuable to very valuable. Last, reflective opportunities are limited for a wide range of reasons in any context.

In the final phase of analysis, the entire body of data, including interview and observation summaries and transcripts, was reviewed once more, keeping in mind the analyzed instances (drawn from participants' storied examples) and the themes revealed in analysis (derived from the researcher's interpretation). In this final pass through the data the researcher's and participants' interpretations of events were compared. Collections of their own reported and observed instances were made available to participants for verification. Results of analysis were presented verbally to participants, who were invited to comment. Where applicable, presentation of the results was revised according to the teachers' input.

SUMMARY

This chapter has provided an overview of the study informing this book. It discussed the dimensions of reflection relevant in studying teachers' experience. It also described the research process for drawing conclusions about reflection in teaching. The research yielded the cases of reflection presented in the chapters that follow, as well as an understanding of reflection that can help practitioners support it in teaching and teacher learning. We now enter into the worlds of the four accomplished teachers, starting with the context most familiar in their daily professional lives: the context of their schools.

Chapter Four

Reflecting in School:
The Professional Context

OVERVIEW OF THIS SECTION:
MULTIPLE MATTERS FOR REFLECTION

Schools can be ideal venues for reflection. Research supports the idea of teachers' reflective, professional learning taking place in schools (Ball & Cohen, 1999; Darling-Hammond & McLaughlin, 1995; Darling-Hammond & Sykes, 1999; Smylie, 1995). Where else can you find groups of experienced teachers with their materials at hand, as well as multiple matters for reflection at their fingertips—from student achievement to issues of equity to the challenges of a high-stakes environment? To find teachers reflecting on their practice, we should surely begin by looking in schools.

Or should we? Research tells us this seemingly ideal setting for reflection may actually *work against* it (Fullan, 1991; Sarason, 1990, 1996). Despite the matters demanding attention in schools, the complexity of those matters—not to mention the overloaded nature of teachers' schedules and the chronic absence of time—can make reflection difficult to achieve. The busyness of school life and the sometimes frenetic pace of teaching hardly seem welcoming to an activity associated with slowing down, contemplating, and thinking earnestly. Do teachers actually find ways to reflect day to day? Where and when do they do so and how effective is the process?

This section of the book explores the paradox of reflecting in schools, the "professional context." This chapter presents teachers' general perspectives on school-based reflection. Subsequent chapters include cases from typical events in daily school life: staff meetings, department meetings, teacher evaluation, informal collegial meetings, and the context of teaching. The last chapter reviews key themes of reflection in schools.

A FRAMEWORK FOR LEARNING FROM THE CASES

Cases of reflection in schools include a wide range of situations. In some cases, reflection seems badly needed, but not welcome. In others, reflection is intended but not realized. In still others, reflection occurs, but seems meaningless. In the best-case scenarios, reflection is both present and meaningful, with a contribution to teaching and learning. To sort through this mixed bag of cases, an organizing frame is needed. Asking a set of questions after each case can allow us to understand reflection across multiple circumstances: Did reflection take place? What supported or hindered reflection? How was the reflection valuable to teaching? Let us now explore these questions.

Did Reflection Take Place?

The first question that will be asked of each case is, "Did reflection take place?" To answer this question, we can rely on our established definition of reflection:

> looking back on experience in a way that informs practice, learning in the midst of practice, and/or making informed and intelligent decisions about what to do, when to do it, and why it should be done. (Shulman, 1987; Richert, 1990; Schön, 1983)

This definition spans the boundaries of reflection, making it useful for thinking about all kinds of reflection in teaching, even though it may appear different from one case to the next. For instance, one teacher's reflection may be prompted by a structured activity in a staff meeting; another may involve informal musing after a lesson. The two scenarios differ greatly and each may count as reflection. Applying this definition to each situation allows us to recognize reflection when we see it and makes it possible to look across all of the activities in a school and ask, "Is this situation reflective?"

What Supported or Hindered Reflection?

The second question that will be asked of each case is, "What supported or hindered reflection?" This is an important question, for it can help us understand *why* reflection occurs *when* it does and *how*. When reflection does take place, we can ask, "What happened to make this situation supportive of reflection?" When it does not, we can ask, "Why not?" and "How could this situation become more reflective?"—two more questions that help us learn from teachers about how to support reflection in schools.

How Was the Reflection Valuable to Teaching?

Besides identifying reflection and analyzing the conditions that support it, one more question will be asked: "How was the reflection valuable to teaching?" This question assesses each case from a different perspective. To illustrate, imagine a teacher at his desk thinking about a struggling student in his class. To the teacher, the activity may be valuable reflection. To someone walking by, the teacher may appear idle. Asking, "Is this activity valuable?" we can only answer, "It depends." It depends on whether we ask the teacher or the passerby. It depends on whether the teacher can work on the problem for as long as it takes. It depends on whether he can resolve or improve the situation. In each case, an assessment will be made whether the activity adds value to teaching or is, in effect, a waste of time.

What Can We Learn from Each Case?

Because each case is unique and offers different opportunities for learning about reflection, one more question will be asked: "What can we learn from this case?" This section highlights specific characteristics of situations that bear on reflection. This makes it possible not only to identify and analyze various situations involving reflection, but also to discover *why* reflection occurs and *how it could* occur as a valuable aspect of teaching.

The cases in this section, drawn from typical events in daily school life, all have the potential to incorporate reflection (Darling-Hammond & McLaughlin, 1995). Each chapter presents a set of cases and explores them in terms of three central questions: Did reflection take place? What supported or hindered reflection? How was reflection valuable to teaching? Looking across the cases with the aid of these questions will reveal insights about fostering reflective teaching. Before exploring the teachers' experiences, however, it is important to understand the teachers' collective thoughts on reflection. What do *they* say reflection is and how do they believe it helps them in their teaching? Their insights provide our first glimpse into the nature of reflection in schools.

THE NATURE OF REFLECTION
IN THE CONTEXT OF SCHOOLS

To this point, the discussion has relied on research to tell us what reflection is and what it achieves. But the nuances of reflection become evident when talking to teachers. To gain a clearer awareness of what reflection means to teachers in their everyday work, the discussion will turn now to their definitions of reflection and its importance in schools.

A Definition of Reflection

Asked to define reflection in their own words, the teachers responded in similar ways:

Underwood: Reflection is looking back on what you've done. . . . It's discovering what you can improve upon and what you don't ever want to do again.

Green: Reflection means to look at actually what you do and figure out why it worked or why it didn't. . . . You look and see how you would change it.

King: Reflection means pausing or stopping, . . . looking back at something and seeing what you see. You don't look at it in the rush of the moment, you look at it in the pause.

Nichols: Reflection is being thoughtful about what one does and why. . . . When we look back on what it is that we've done, we see it a little differently. We give it time and space.

Consistently, the teachers identified reflection as a process of "looking" — holding a situation still for a moment, pausing to see it, and taking in the meaning. Additionally, the teachers all noted that reflection involves some kind of judgment, an evaluation of the situation that they've paused to see.

Finally, several of their definitions imply change. The words "improve," "change," and "see it differently" indicate that by nature reflection opens up the possibility that a situation may require new action on the part of the teacher.

Because this section will be examining specific events of teachers' school days, it may seem that reflection itself is an "event." In fact, it often seems to be. However, one of the teachers also noted that, for her, reflecting was an ongoing, never-ending process. "I make mistakes every day. Every day there [are] ways I could do it better. Every day I think, 'If I'd only done *this.*'" This remark reveals another dimension of reflection: that even though it may or may not consistently happen, the *possibility* for it always exists.

The Importance of Reflection

According to the teachers, reflection is an essential aspect of practice. Their ideas about its importance fell into three categories: improvement, discovery, and survival.

Improvement. The teachers all asserted that reflection is important for improving practice—a stated goal of reform efforts and many activities for teachers (Fullan, 1991; Fullan & Miles, 1992; Sarason, 1990). King explained the relationship between reflection and improvement: "If you want to change teaching, reflection's very important. Because without reflection—[and] this is not particularly teaching, [it's] any human activity—people do exactly what they've experienced." Her opinion is supported by research, which verifies that without new images and ideas for their practice, teachers do what they witnessed teachers doing as students (Lortie, 1975). Given evolving views of effective teaching (Hawley & Valli, 1999), ideas about what and how students should learn (Gardner, 2000; Sizer & Sizer, 1999), and the ever-diversifying needs of modern students (Ladson-Billings, 1999), for teachers to repeat behavior they encountered as students is not only ineffective, it's counterproductive. In contrast, reflection elicits positive change. As Underwood put it, "If you're looking to really change things, you really need to take the time to reflect on what's good and bad already." According to the teachers, one important reason for reflecting is continual improvement.

Discovery. Another reason the teachers believed reflection was important involved discovery. Without reflecting, Underwood asserted, it would be impossible for teachers to be sure whether their approaches to teaching were effective, "Because we haven't sat down and talked about them and said, 'Did we do a good job?'" That sense of doing a good job was important to all of the teachers. In Green's words, "If you don't reflect, how do you know you're doing a good job? And if you don't know you're not doing a good job, you've got another problem!" But the problem to which Green refers is not just a problem for the individual teacher—it's a problem for schools and the students. When teachers aren't aware of their effectiveness and don't engage in discovery to *become* more aware, poor practice persists—a situation schools can little afford.

Survival. In addition to improvement and discovery, one of the teachers identified a third reason for reflection: survival. King explained that without taking the time to think about the circumstances of schooling, the job would be impossibly complex. "In the modern public school, at least, there [are] way too many kids and way too much curriculum and way too much change *not* to reflect." In King's experience, the dynamics of teaching demand reflection as part of the job.

SUMMARY

When considering reflection in schools, the teachers believed that reflection was an ongoing process of looking at their practice in order to decide whether their teaching was successful, to improve it when necessary, and to make sense of a dynamic environment. But the reality of reflection in school life turned out to be much less straightforward.

The next several chapters illustrate this point as they look at cases of the teachers' experiences with reflection in schools. As we shall see, tremendous variation existed in the teachers' experiences. Some activities made no room for reflection at all. Some invited reflection but could not sustain it, and some involved reflection but didn't affect practice. Other reflective activities seemed effective and did help the teachers in their teaching. More often than not, reflection in the school context was limited, and, at times, it was even pointless. The next several chapters examine cases of reflection that run this gamut of effectiveness. A discussion after each case identifies what worked and what didn't in supporting reflection and what can be learned about reflection in schools.

Chapter Five

Staff Meetings

When school staff members get together, what do they talk about? Staff meetings in education, as in many professions, serve multiple purposes. They offer an efficient way to dispense information. They provide the opportunity to inform everyone of events at the school, the schedule, and the priorities. They can provide a forum for questions and discussion about current concerns of staff members and administrators alike. Given these purposes, making reflection part of a staff meeting makes sense. Using staff meetings in this way has been suggested by researchers and policy makers who encourage educators to make such meetings substantive (Darling-Hammond & McLaughlin, 1995; Hill et al., 1997). But how reflection fares in the context of a staff meeting depends on a number of factors. In this chapter, we observe two extremes: one staff meeting in which reflection was welcome and another in which it was not. As we shall see, although one meeting was more effective than the other, neither situation was ideal.

CASES OF STAFF MEETINGS

In all of the teachers' schools, staff meetings were either lecture-format meetings or meetings for special projects. Both types contained multiple matters for reflection, but only one offered the opportunity to address these matters, as seen in the following two cases. This first case illustrates a lecture-format meeting at Underwood's school. The purpose was to satisfy a district requirement to inform teachers of the discipline policy.

From the beginning to the end of the meeting, it is clear reflection was not on the agenda.

Case #1: A Lecture-Format Staff Meeting

At Northern High School, students are dismissed at noon to allow the staff to meet. About 150 staff members gather in the school cafeteria, filling it with noise. Impatient, a teacher looks at the clock and mutters, "I just wasted eight minutes. Come on."

The meeting begins with the principal speaking into a microphone at the front of the room. In his opening line, he apologizes for requiring a necessary evil—a policy-laden, district-mandated presentation on student discipline. For an hour and a half, he conducts a lecture on "Discipline How-To's." Topics include varieties of suspension, students' rights, disciplinary policies, and a behavior-management multistep process.

Teachers respond in a number of ways. Some sit quietly, listening. Others emit an air of resistance by working on other activities, like the student teacher hunched over a stack of papers, grading. Many sit back with their arms tightly folded, commenting to their colleagues as the presenter goes through transparencies on the overhead screen. Periodically, teachers call out jokes showing they take this lecture lightly. When the principal announces that corporal punishment is "humiliation and embarrassment," a teacher jokes, "But humiliation and embarrassment's okay, right?" Everyone laughs.

Finally, the principal ends with an apologetic acknowledgment that experienced teachers might not have needed to hear this lecture on discipline, but that district policy and the hiring of new teachers made it necessary. The lecture being over, teachers raise other issues. In the remaining fifteen minutes of the meeting, a number of topics are thrown out for discussion in rapid succession, including updates on gang activity, wasted resources, communication failure, and the emotional abuse of teachers. As topics dwindle and teachers start milling around, the meeting is over.

Debriefing the case. What can we learn from this staff meeting on student discipline that relates to reflection? After all, it seems clear that little reflection took place. Yet, we can learn from this nonexample about the reality of schools as settings in which reflection must exist.

Did reflection take place? Unfortunately, this case is instructive as a circumstance that prohibits reflection. The principal's apology for boring teachers, the mandated nature of the agenda, and the lecture format all suggest that reflection wasn't invited to this meeting. No opportunities for reflection were built into the agenda; teachers were expected to accept or at least listen to the information without comment, then squeeze in comments on remaining issues (and there were many) in a sentence or two at the end.

What supported or hindered reflection? Aspects of this meeting—especially the severity of topics raised at the end—show a desperate need for reflection, although it was largely hindered by the format. A number of issues seemed to warrant, but didn't receive, consideration. The lecture was designed to *tell* teachers what to do about discipline instead of *asking* why discipline problems persisted. This approach communicates acceptance of the issue as simply the way things are, whereas reflection would emphasize change.

With a few simple changes, the meeting could have been altered to support reflection and potentially improve discipline problems. Consider how the meeting would have been different had the principal raised reflective questions, such as:

- What can staff and administration learn about their effectiveness in reaching students by thinking deeply about discipline issues and policies?
- Who is the policy meant to serve and is it serving them?
- Is the district discipline policy effective? Does it actually curb discipline issues?
- How is discipline affecting teaching, learning, and overall school effectiveness?

These questions all offer entrances into reflection that could have informed the school, its teachers, its leaders on the subject of discipline, and perhaps even some of the issues underlying it—such as student frustration, lack of engagement, and disempowerment. But no room for these questions existed in the meeting; instead, the lecture was conducted with an acceptance of the problems as a part of school life. Issues were raised but not discussed; both they and the teachers were dismissed after a jam-packed meeting.

How was reflection valuable to teaching? A meeting needn't be reflective to hold value; certainly lectures can motivate people to learn and grow in their teaching. Yet, in this meeting, this wasn't the case. To Underwood, who spent the time filling out forms for the swim team, this meeting seemed to hold little meaning at all. In subsequent conversations about reflection in his school, he never mentioned it again.

What can we learn from this case? What we learn from this case is that staff meetings can easily preclude whole-staff reflection, simply by being conducted as they have stereotypically been, as opportunities for information dissemination. But the *need* for reflection, seeping through in the form of comments at the end of the meeting, allows us to glimpse a different approach—one in which a staff looks at a situation, reflects on it, decides what's working and what isn't (and for whom), and takes conscientious steps toward improving instead of simply perpetuating a situation. Such a purpose would raise the bar on staff meetings, creating a time for a staff to tackle, not just manage, the issues.

The good news is that even this staff meeting, and staff meetings in general, do hold some promise for reflection. Staff meetings are a typical mode of operation in schools; the structure is already in place for administrators, teachers, and support staff to get together and discuss school issues. Moreover, issues impacting schools are well known to teachers and researchers, further enhancing the opportunity in such meetings to discuss issues of the greatest priority. What is needed, then, is a kind of meeting that focuses on issues while also taking advantage of the many minds collected in the room. What is needed is a kind of meeting that addresses ideas in the interest of real change; and real change requires reflection and a deeper level of involvement by teachers.

In fairness, the meeting in this case was not intended to generate reflective thinking, and certainly not all meetings will. But one must wonder what kind of improvements might occur if staff meetings were to move away from lecture and toward reflection. Examples of such meetings do exist. In fact, one such meeting actually took place at Underwood's school—in the same room, with the same group of people, but for a different kind of purpose. The second case of a school staff meeting provides an educative contrast in which reflection *is* on the agenda.

Case #2: A Special Project Staff Meeting

Good news has arrived at Northern High School: the school has received a new grant. Administrators arrange a whole-staff meeting to explore the possibilities afforded by the money. The principal cancels classes so that the entire faculty—teachers, administrators, counselors, and classified staff—can generate thoughts for restructuring this school of 1,800 students into smaller schools within the school. For a whole afternoon, the faculty concentrates on ideas for creating a more personalized environment. The activities of the meeting are largely reflective, as teachers journal individually, share ideas in discussion, and produce summaries of ideas about what personalizing a high school would mean, what such schools are like for students and teachers, and what their school is already doing to reach students.

One section of the meeting illustrates the flavor of the agenda. In this half-hour block of time, the teachers are asked to free associate the word "personalize." Then they are each given a sheet of paper with a single question at the top: "What will it be like for students who attend a highly personalized high school?" For ten minutes, teachers individually write and reflect on the question. They then share ideas at their tables and create composite lists on butcher paper to be hung around the room.

At Underwood's table, teachers focus first on reporting ideas for personalizing the school and writing them into bulleted points. Emerging examples include:

- *Students are not lost in system.*
- *Teachers get to know students long term, small scale.*
- *Students and teachers are invested in their success in school.*
- *Students believe they're valued.*

Gradually, the talk takes the shape of collaboration as the teachers exchange ideas, question each other, and spot themes in their comments.

Drawing on their own experience, the teachers debate ideas before agreeing on a common language for the chart. In one of these exchanges, one teacher suggests creating school "houses" based on career pathways. Another teacher worries aloud that this could turn into tracking. She replies to her colleague, "I don't know about that option, because you can get into tracking and students being grouped. I really am against that." In a respectful and thoughtful tone, the teachers deliberate on the issue for a moment, then arrive at the conclusion that flexible pathways could both prepare students for a career and allow them to easily change paths if they wish.

The teachers also consider ways to spend more time with students than the current quarter system allows, ways to offer students curricular options without overburdening teachers, and ways to connect with students not involved in teams and clubs. After a sincere effort to create a meaningful list, one of the teachers posts it on the wall with the other groups'. In the break that follows, teachers all over the room read each others' lists. When the meeting resumes, the principal explains that all of the ideas on the posters will inform the design team leading changes associated with the grant. Overall, the meeting has a distinctly reflective tone, as teachers use their experience to inform the project, giving suggestions about what to do to personalize schools and why.

Debriefing the case. What can we learn from this staff meeting on personalizing the school—such a contrast to the lecture-based meeting on student discipline in the previous case? This meeting differs strikingly from the first case in at least two significant ways: reflection is planned into the agenda and it is supported by the activities in the meeting. The result is a more high-powered meeting with the potential to impact the schools' success.

Did reflection take place? Reflection was an explicit part of this meeting. The purpose of the meeting was to actually seek teachers' input and to create activities to generate that input. Moreover, time was dedicated that was appropriate to the purpose. The students were excused for the day so that the faculty as a whole could come together to discuss at length what would improve the learning experience—a tradeoff that shortened instruction time in the short term, but had the potential to improve instructional effectiveness in the long term. Even the arrangement of the room was designed to foster reflection: teachers sat in collaborative groups at round tables with teachers and staff members from around the school and they were invited to talk and share ideas as a way of contributing to the purpose, which was to inform the grant process and make their huge school feel smaller. Accepting change, discovering how the school is doing, and improving where improvement seems needed—all three of the reasons to reflect identified by teachers earlier in this section of the book—were a part of this meeting.

What supported or hindered reflection? In addition to planning reflection into the agenda, this meeting was significant in a second, additional way. Not only was reflection invited, it was actually taught. Returning momentarily to the overview of reflection presented in chapter 2, it is not just the presence of reflection that counts, but the quality as well. The administrators who arranged this staff meeting carefully planned questions to guide the discussion. Several of the questions asked were reflective by nature: What is working in the school already that makes it feel "personal," and what needs to change to improve it? Who would such changes affect if they went into place, and how? What are all of the different options available for personalizing the school and how do they compare? Importantly, the time allotted for group discussion of the questions actually allowed teachers to practice reflecting together. As seen in Underwood's group, the teachers approached some hot topics—tracking and student isolation, to name just two. The respect with which two teachers disagreed with each other and the fairness with which they weighed opinions were both examples for the other teachers at the table, and they set a reflective tone that improved the effectiveness of the conversation.

Thus, what we learn from this case is that staff meetings can be ideal settings for reflection. This is especially true (1) when reflection is linked to the purpose of the meeting, (2) when the activities of the meeting support reflective thought, (3) when structures (like questions, physical arrangements, and time) are designed to support, teach, and allow teachers to practice reflection, and (4) when the issues go deep enough to address the challenging side of change. All of these were present in this case.

How was reflection valuable to teaching? Surprisingly, Underwood's perspective reveals that incorporating reflection into meetings isn't enough. Despite a general feeling among teachers that the meeting was effective and reflective, Underwood was skeptical of its success. Specifically, he wondered what would happen as time went on.

Now, we'll take the next step, start to instigate some of these things. But will they plan [to reflect on the progress]? Will they stop [periodically] and say, does this work or not? . . . If it doesn't work, it'll be five years down the road [before] we finally sit down and reflect on it and go, oh, hey, that didn't work.

Underwood's suggestion would be to stop along the way and assess what was and was not working. But, he stressed, "That hardly ever happens." To illustrate, Underwood referenced several experiences in his ten years of teaching that fueled this concern—including one in which the school had received a large grant and kicked it off with a reflective whole-school meeting, just like the one in this case, then suffered through a series of mistakes in subsequent years. Even though reflective activity took place as part of the new grant to personalize the school, the long-term significance of the event seemed uncertain to at least one teacher who had been down this road before.

What can we learn from this case? This case presents two lessons about reflection. First, it can effectively be structured into whole-staff meetings with benefits for school improvement. Second, such reflection can be ineffectual unless it is a habitual part of the change process, not just a one-time event.

SUMMARY

The cases above reveal two themes regarding reflection in the school context. On one hand, some staff meetings provide little if any room for reflection. In such meetings, arising issues may signal a need for reflection, but the opportunity to discuss them can easily be missed in favor of another purpose that may or may not relate to student learning.

On the other hand, special efforts can be made in staff meetings to expressly initiate reflection. Activities can be designed to guide teachers in thinking about what is going on in the school and why. Yet, these opportunities won't necessarily be meaningful to the teachers—particularly if they expect the efforts to be short-lived. Even meaningful opportunities can backfire in the long term and leave teachers feeling cautious if not downright bitter when circumstances force a withdrawal from projects they believe to have been effective (Fullan, 1991). In both of the examples from Underwood's school, administrators initiated change, but their efforts were thwarted by circumstances related to the change process; they seemed to seek reflective practice but not to sustain the structures to support it. It seems that to be truly effective, reflection must be more than a single event. To be truly effective, reflection must become an enduring ethic over time. Does the same pattern hold true for other kinds of school meetings? In the next chapter, we witness more efforts to foster reflection, this time within the teachers' departments.

Chapter Six

Department Meetings

How do department meetings differ from staff meetings? Like staff meetings, department meetings serve multiple purposes. Teachers share content-based information, align curriculum, and compare ideas about how to teach their subject. They also provide a smaller group setting in which teachers can take on school projects with more room for discussion than typically available in a whole-staff environment. Led by a department head rather than an administrator, these meetings have the potential to bring colleagues together on issues that impact them directly. In such a climate, reflection seems likely: colleagues with similar interests have the chance in a manageable group to discuss what is important to them. Unfortunately, the reality can be far from this ideal. In fact, the cases in this chapter are characterized less by actual reflection than by missed opportunities.

CASES OF DEPARTMENT MEETINGS

This chapter features three department meetings with mixed results for reflection. Unlike in their staff meetings, the teachers did initiate reflective activities within their departments. Unfortunately, their attempts were often thwarted and reflection struggled to survive. In all of the cases, teachers took turns talking rapidly and covered a number of topics, often carrying on several conversations at once in a race against the clock.

Department meetings in the teachers' schools usually followed a similar format. Groups of ten to twelve people met in a classroom to discuss a given agenda set by an administrator or the department chair. The case that follows is a representative snapshot of a typical meeting in Green's department. Given the issues on the agenda, reflection seemed needed, but given the structure, no reflection took place.

Case #1: A Typical Department Meeting

In the math department at Southern High School, Green and her colleagues attend a monthly meeting. Teachers listen dutifully as the chair spends the half-hour time slot reporting back from other meetings. She shares what happened at the School Leadership meeting, attended by department chairs and administrators only. Her report features a number of issues, including a $50,000 district budget cut due to underenrollment (even though this school houses 1,600 students in a building built for 1,200) and a substitute shortage (which has forced teachers to cover classes during planning time). Teachers respond with objections, but their reactions don't get very far. They know that when it comes to school policy and decisions, their hands are tied. At exactly the end of the half hour, the teachers rush out of the room. It's the end of the contracted day.

Debriefing the case. This glimpse into Green's meeting illustrates a typical scenario: teachers are asked to listen and not to question information. What can this case teach us about the role of reflection in department meetings? As with Underwood's staff meeting on discipline, we can learn from this nonexample of reflection about why reflection doesn't seem welcome.

Did reflection take place? In this case, reflection did not occur. Why? First, this meeting fits into a bureaucratic structure in which information is passed down the line from administrators to department chairs to teachers. Second, just enough time is allotted for the purpose, and no more. Third, decisions, regardless of their impact on the teachers or student learning, are announced to teachers after the fact. Finally, the teachers themselves avoid reflective discussion on these issues; after all, the situation is what it is. As a result of this format for the meeting, reflection simply doesn't have a chance.

What supported or hindered reflection? Besides the obvious discouragement of discussion imposed by the meeting format, reflection in this case is hindered by a lack of acknowledgment that issues warrant discussion and input from the teachers. And yet the issues loom large. Consider the reflective questions that *could* have been asked at this meeting. Some questions would have helped the teachers discover more about the issue:

• What impact will the budget cut have on the school?
• What will happen to the teachers' classes as a result?

Other questions could have helped them improve the situation:

• How can teachers make the most of a bad situation to protect student learning?
• What instructional strategies suit large class sizes in an overpopulated school?

Finally, teachers could have asked the most critical questions of all—the ones about the survival of schools and teachers when resources are so tight:

• What structures and systems alleviate large classes despite high numbers of students?
• And, most importantly, what implications does the budget cut have for student learning? What are the underlying assumptions and how are they driving the school's direction? What should these assumptions be?

These questions would take a complex subject and open it up for creative solutions and, possibly, the avoidance of a crisis. Similar questions could be asked on the substitute shortage and help teachers discover and explore the problem, compare options to manage the situation as best they can, attend to the critical survival of teachers' time, and protect the quality of learning despite the challenge posed by the shortage. A change in both the structure of the meeting and the implication that such questions are welcome would support reflection, teaching, and learning in times of scarce resources and limited space.

Answers to such reflective questions are easily found. And the responsibility for solving such societal issues as underfunding, overcrowding, and the diminishing pool of substitutes doesn't rest with teachers. Nevertheless, when schools and districts move directly from problem to solution with little time for reflection—as glimpsed in the postdecision involvement of the teachers—the results may be detrimental to both teachers and their students. Teachers are impacted and yet have no voice in the matter.

How was reflection valuable to teaching? Discussing her reaction to the department meeting, Green dismissed its importance with a shrug. She suggested that the meetings had taken a turn for the worse and that they had been more valuable when they were reflective. When Green had chaired the meetings in the past, talking about *teaching* was part of the agenda. "We used to spend time at the department meetings sharing information [about] teaching activities," she moaned. But times had changed and the department meetings had become less about subject-specific issues and more about administrative alignment. Green's belief that her department meetings weren't particularly reflective and her expressed sense of loss over the substantive, teaching-related conversations she used to have with departmental colleagues made it seem important for other activities in the school to make room for teaching-related conversations. But asked whether the kinds of reflection she wanted to see happen ever did occur ("Are there other times when you do talk about the kinds of things you used to when you were department chair?"), she answered with an unequivocal "No."

What can we learn from this case? Ironically, this nonreflective meeting has something important to teach us about reflection. The assumptions behind the content and structure of department meetings communicate clearly when reflection is not welcome. Getting these messages, teachers may logically avoid tackling hard issues, accept their roles as mere information recipients, and never contribute to improvement on hard issues. However, Green's remembrance of past reflective meetings suggested that other models actually invite reflection, with benefits for teachers and their schools.

The department meeting at Green's school was not set up to foster reflection; its goals were purely administrative. For the meetings to become reflective would require not only a different structure, but also a different function altogether—one based on the goals and purposes of the department, perhaps, or instructional approaches to teaching the content. We see an example of this from another school—another case of a department meeting that *could* have been reflective. This case, drawn from King's experience, shows a department meeting in which the teachers considered how to teach their subject in light of the goals of the school.

Case #2: A Special Project Department Meeting

*On a teacher workday, administrators in King's school call for depart-
ments to discuss school goals related to the state assessment. King and
her social studies colleagues are to determine ways to help the school
meet those goals. The activity structured for the purpose requires reflection, but the teachers hardly take it seriously.*

*When the eight teachers have gathered in a circle, the department chair
tells them their task: to recommend goals to help implement the state assessment, focusing on the school's emphasis (reading). He holds up a
chart, saying, "This is the template I'm supposed to submit. I told them
we've been working hard on it!" Having "already devoted 2 minutes of
brainpower to it," he announces, "this is what I came up with: 'reading
for critical content.'" The teachers agree and fill out the rest of the chart,
shouting out responses in typical standards lingo as the chair calls out the
questions.*

"What is needed to make this goal be successful?" he reads.

"Student and parent involvement!" they cry.

"How will we know if we've achieved it?"

"Self-assessment and student participation!"

*Having filled out the chart, the chair announces a plan. "What I
thought I'd do is to just type this up as if we've all had our breakout sessions, brainstormed and discussed goals, and come back together. . . . I'll
type it all up for us and bring it to the department chair meeting." With
this approach, the department covers the task in a short period of time and
gives the chair something to report at his meeting later in the day.*

Debriefing the case. This case illustrates a well-intentioned activity
gone awry. School administrators wanted teachers to reflect on goals in an
effort to align the state assessment, the school goals, and the department's
focus. The activity invited input from teachers, with plenty of room for reflection on what they could do to improve student learning. Yet, at the department chair's suggestion, the teachers in King's department managed
to avoid this process. Nevertheless, they fulfilled the assignment they
were given. As a result, the meeting was both a success and a failure in
terms of reflection.

Did reflection take place? In a sense, the teachers' response to the task
was reflective; after all, they did identify what they were doing and why

in order to meet school goals. But this approach was unquestionably inauthentic. As the department chair explained, "What [administrators] don't understand is our jobs have gotten so complicated, we need the time to actually *do* the work. Pressed for time and juggling responsibilities, the teachers didn't prioritize the reflection that was structured into the meeting.

What supported or hindered reflection? One key factor in this situation worked against reflection: resistance to the assumptions of the activity. King explained her view of the problem. She saw a kind of resistance emerging consciously or unconsciously from the teachers: an implicit and informed decision not to reflect on the goals. First, King explained her thoughts about this kind of meeting in general and the teachers' response:

> I think what [the administration is] doing is shepherding us to try to make sure each department is squarely faced to the [state assessment] issues and doing something in the department to try to address either skills that are clearly demanded or areas of weakness that clearly exist. That's what they want.

Then she expressed her opinion of this motive, calling it "both reasonable and unreasonable." She saw it as reasonable with respect to public perception; she believed that the staff was invested in the state test to the extent that they didn't want to "look bad" when the scores were "plastered all over the newspaper." However, she saw it as unreasonable in the sense that the school was strong by many measures, some of which were more important to teachers than test scores. Resistance to reflecting on goals linked to the state test related to resistance to the state test itself. In King's view, the faculty didn't "buy in" to the idea that the state test was "a good test, or even a good idea." In short, one factor working against reflection in this meeting was the teachers' resistance to the assumptions of the task.

How was reflection valuable to teaching? Any reflection that did occur in this meeting can only be called superficial. In minutes, the teachers aligned their existing practice with the school goals and essentially dismissed the importance of the state assessment that those goals were meant to support. Rather than reflect on and change their practice in accordance with the task, the teachers simply satisfied its surface requirements and returned to teaching as usual. King called this "an investment in mediocrity," since current practices weren't always the best, but she also acknowledged that one reason teachers resisted changing their practice was that reform efforts tended to come and go, and teachers had developed the sense that this reform, too, would pass.

What can we learn from this case? From this single example of a department meeting, we learn that simply structuring a reflective activity does not guarantee the resulting reflection. Even setting aside special time for the purpose doesn't necessarily buy careful thought. Teachers must also see genuine value in the activity and believe it contributes positively to their teaching. Lacking this, they can easily dismiss the activity. Reflection apparently can't be "required." Does this mean teachers never reflect on the goals and issues of their school? Certainly not, as we see in the next case.

In case #2, teachers sidestepped reflection to satisfy an agenda. The next case shows the opposite scenario: teachers sidestepping the agenda to reflect on a matter of importance. The case shows a different side to the teachers in King's department.

Case #3: Between Agenda Items in Meetings

As usual, the Eastern High School social studies department attacks its agenda with vigor, ticking off administrative items with speed, to get them quickly back to their classrooms. As they fill out a form listing department strategies for improving student learning, the issue of student study habits is raised.

Concerned, King wants to discuss this issue at length, but her colleagues plow on through the form. King labors to get the attention of her colleagues to make her point: students are lacking critical note-taking skills. She wants to discuss a plan to improve their proficiency by reinstating a plan to give students study packets—a system that had formerly worked.

Misreading her sincerity, the department chair pipes, "That sounds good! I'll put that in," and scribbles her suggestion on the form.

In frustration, King tries to shift the conversation. "If we actually seriousd up a bit," she starts, asserting that she wants to be heard. She persists in describing the issue and finally gets her colleagues to listen. At last, they join her in discussing ways to improve note-taking skills and provide students with the study packet King suggests.

Together, the teachers realize that they all recognize a note-taking problem, but aren't sure about how best to attack it. Using their experience to inform the issue, teachers voice some pros and cons. One teacher remembers how the students responded to the packets the first time they were used at the school: "The kids hated it." Another agrees, but argues, "It's a pain, but it works! And it makes a big difference for the kids." Around the circle, teachers pitch in ideas about how the study packets could look, share ideas from their classrooms, and even bring in sample packets from schools at which they have previously taught. As a direct result of King's initiative, the teachers find themselves reflecting together by deliberating on an issue with potential to improve student learning. Having genuinely considered a problem they share, King and her colleagues decide to persuade administrators to reinstate the study packets schoolwide.

Debriefing the case. This case includes familiar themes. The department meeting had an administrative agenda, teachers were flying through it at record speed, and reflection had to fight for the floor. In contrast to the other cases in this chapter, however, King managed to squeeze in a question right in the middle of the meeting ("How can we support students' note-taking skills?") and get her colleagues to reflect on it.

Did reflection take place? Given the exchange of ideas to solve an issue of student learning, King's attempts to foster reflection succeeded. The particular kind of reflection in which they engaged might be called deliberative, as the teachers debated the pros and cons of different instructional strategies. In so doing, they were able to determine which kind of study packet would work best for the students and propose the idea as one way to promote school goals—not just to fill up the list that held them accountable for the meeting, but to actually improve student learning. The department meeting thus became an impromptu forum for reflection, squeezed into the agenda between the official tasks.

What supported or hindered reflection? In this case, although the department's tendency to speed through agendas could have hindered the reflection, King's assertiveness nevertheless made it happen. King reported that such assertiveness was sometimes a necessity in her department's fast-paced meetings. "Sometimes people throw things out, but they get lost. Sometimes you have to say [she pounds her fist on the table], I really want this done! I'm serious!" With persistence, she prompted her colleagues to reflect on the issue at least long enough to take action on an issue of student learning. Thinking about what supports reflection more generally, King shows us the value of a strong department member ready to take a stand on important issues. Without such assertion, important problems may be overlooked, if not ignored.

How was reflection valuable to teaching? How valuable is this kind of reflection? The answer is unclear. To King, the issue was important, suggesting that the reflection might have been meaningful. However, whether any practical impact came from the reflective conversation was unresolved. After the scene in this case, the department chair took the idea to his department chairs' meeting, where these kinds of decisions were made. Knowing the controversy this apparently benign idea could incite, King explained that it would take months to settle the matter, which would first be "discussed to death."

What can we learn from this case? This case illustrates what can happen when teachers reflect on issues together. But there is another side to this story. Regardless of the severity of the issue, teachers rarely succeeded in encouraging reflection as King did. The issue in King's meeting described above received the teachers' attention, but other instances occurred in which pressing matters simply arose and departed with little notice. In these situations, opportunities to reflect on issues were lost in the midst of the agenda.

For example, teachers in one of King's department meetings angrily discussed the district's failure to renew a teacher's contract without apparent reason. In response, the teacher shrugged and muttered, "I can get [another] job." Another teacher sadly described his students' apathy during his most exciting lesson and he seemed resigned to a belief that public education was "going out with a whimper." More issues that seeped into meeting agendas included questions about printers that didn't work, budget money being taken away, and challenges to art programs that were hard to measure for assessment. In all of these examples, issues vital to teaching and learning lay just under the surface of what could be misconstrued as minor complaints. Lacking King's diligence and her colleagues' responsiveness to the issues, matters that were important enough to be raised didn't get discussed; they were merely described and expediently dismissed.

In department meetings, for teacher after teacher, critical issues like these flowed through conversation like water through a sieve. Raising matters that seemed to warrant attention didn't necessarily prompt reflection. The teachers lamented the troubles they faced in their work, but seemed to lack either the capacity or the inclination to address them.

SUMMARY

In these cases of department meetings, structured opportunities for reflection were more often sought than found. When reflection *was* on the agenda, teachers decided on their own whether the task was worth the effort. When reflection *wasn't* on the agenda, they pushed for attention on topics that couldn't be ignored, but couldn't necessarily be resolved. The story was replicated time and again in every teacher's department.

Regardless of the agenda, in dialogue oddly juxtaposed with efforts to sidestep required reflective tasks, teachers seemed to crave authentic reflection. In between the items of the agenda, a parallel plan was operating in which teachers initiated the chance to talk about their concerns, by presenting problems, promoting suggestions, or raising issues. Between agenda items, deep questions about teaching, education, and learning were brewing, bubbling to the surface long enough to hint at ominous problems, but not long enough to allow for reflection. Thus teachers raised, but didn't deal with, the issues. Instead, they met each other's predicaments with empathy and advice, but rarely a solution. Dilemmas were raised and left hanging. Reflection was minimal but desperately needed, as these matters (and the teachers raising them) practically screamed for attention. Interestingly, the teachers sometimes created special meetings off the administrators' radar screen to deal with such urgent issues. Given more time and more freedom, could teachers find more success with reflection? We will see some results in the next chapter, on informal collegial meetings.

Chapter Seven

Informal Collegial Meetings

What can informal meetings offer that their more formal counterparts cannot? With staff and department meetings reserved for other matters, teachers sometimes create circumstances to reflect together on issues that matter to them. Although these meetings make time and space for reflective opportunities, unlike many school-based meetings, they too present less-than-ideal settings for reflection. As seen in the two cases in this chapter, once again issues are raised and left hanging. However, compared with cases from staff and department meetings, the issues seem at least welcome in these contexts and the teachers seem ready to talk, share, and learn.

CASES OF INFORMAL COLLEGIAL MEETINGS

One informal collegial meeting in which room was made for reflection was Nichols's lunchtime study group. Nichols herself formed this group, in which ten or so teachers voluntarily met weekly to talk about teaching. In previous meetings, they discussed current topics such as schools within schools, general issues such as class size, and specific concerns that the teachers brought up, such as parent contact and failing students. In the following case, the subject of the lunchtime meeting was reflection.

Case #1: A Lunchtime Study Group

Five minutes after the bell rings for lunch, teachers filter into Nichols's classroom. As sandwiches and soup thermoses are unpacked, Nichols re-

minds the group of the day's topic and asks them to share the ways they reflect on their practice.

One of Nichols's colleagues starts the conversation by describing a daily habit of reflecting on her "vision of teaching" during her afternoon jog. Another explains her preference for talking with colleagues, describing challenges she's faced, and asking, "What could I have done better?" A third reports that she attaches sticky notes on her lessons with messages to herself. "This worked really well!" "Held their attention," and "Don't do this again!" are all examples of the little reminders she writes so she will remember from one year to the next how a given lesson went. Without those notes, she adds, she'd "just make the same mistakes again." Other ideas thrown out on the table include journal writing, talking to spouses, and assessing lessons with student teachers. As teachers share their ideas, they joke and tell stories, while Nichols validates their ideas and prompts for more.

When the sharing finally slows, the conversation turns to other matters. Overall, conversation is lively, but bound by the constraints of the lunch hour. Teachers have twenty-five minutes to scramble to the meeting, gobble a lunch, talk as fast as they can, and get back to their rooms by the bell.

Debriefing the case. Nichols's study group served its members in a valuable way, giving them a friendly, collaborative environment in which to jointly address topics of teaching. That the topic of this meeting was reflection can be somewhat misleading, however, and has little bearing on whether the conversation itself was reflective.

Did reflection take place? Even though the *topic* of this meeting was reflection, the *conversation* itself seemed only minimally reflective. Particularly lacking was an effort to go deeper into the topic. The teachers certainly participated in looking back on their practice, but simply described what it was that they did without comparing the benefits of different options or considering how important reflection was to teaching. In order to be truly reflective, the teachers would have also questioned the value of each approach and its resulting effects.

What supported or hindered reflection? In this case, elements of reflective activity were present that were missing in staff and department meetings. Time set aside for discussion, the voluntary nature of the group, the safety of a collegial environment, and the expectation that opinions would be valued all invited reflection in this case.

Still, some other elements may have deepened the reflection. The teachers could have used more time and perhaps a more specific purpose than simply sharing their ideas to really address the topic. They may also have benefited from a structure—a set of questions aimed at deepening their learning, for instance, or a case upon which to reflect—to guide their reflection beyond description to more consequential forms of thought.

How was the reflection valuable to teaching? In this rushed and somewhat casual group meeting, whether the teachers actually found the experience meaningful was impossible to tell. Only individual teachers would know if the conversation informed their practice. Certainly they may have chosen to experiment with their colleagues' ways of reflecting—or they may have simply confirmed that they liked their own approach. Yet, the very fact that they met regularly suggested that the teachers found the meetings valuable enough to work through lunch for the sake of reflection, whatever the topic.

What can we learn from this case? Nichols's study group makes an important point for reflection. Teachers themselves may be the people most capable of designing collegial interactions; such meetings may even be the most conducive to authentic discussion. However, even the most experienced teachers can benefit from strategies designed to foster their reflection. Nevertheless, it should be noted that this teacher-created discussion group, though it could have gone even further in its reflection, was the one of the few times reflection was explicitly discussed among teachers as a topic of importance.

In other, less-structured forms of collegial interaction, the teachers reflected with networks of their colleagues, as seen in the following case. These networks became important when teachers wanted to communicate about issues over the course of several days. The following example occurred when Underwood received news of a new district policy that would directly affect him and his colleagues.

Case #2: Networks of Colleagues

Early one fall, Underwood and his colleagues receive a memo announcing a new policy prohibiting the use of acetic anhydride—an ingredient in one of the students' favorite labs. Underwood's frustration is palpable as he thinks about the memo:

Risk management sent us a memo yesterday with a two-page list of chemicals that we can no longer have. That's it. That was the memo. It said, "You have until Thanksgiving to get rid of the following chemicals" . . . two of which are in our favorite lab. We make aspirin. It's an organic chem lab. . . . Very valuable. It uses a chemical called acetic anhydride, which is a very dangerous chemical. We dispense it in a fume hood, and we warn the kids very much. In the twenty-four years the lab has been part of the curriculum, absolutely no one's gotten hurt.

Straining to contain his anger, Underwood accuses district administration of "typical hypocrisy" for making decisions without asking teachers about the impact on student learning—despite a district policy that people affected by a decision are invited to help make it. He growls through clenched teeth, "Why don't they ask us?"—a question he and his colleagues are deciding how to address as they meet daily to reflect on the issue.

Over the course of several weeks, the chemistry teachers huddle over this issue and crossly consider their case. Underwood summarizes one of their meetings:

We're thinking of just countering with our own risk-management plan. We've identified what we consider to be the dangerous things in the classroom. First, the classroom's designed for twenty-eight students. There are thirty to thirty-two in that class now. Second, the ventilation has never worked properly. We've complained about it for ten years, and they've never done anything about it. And third, there's no time for teachers to really, truly go through all of the chemicals and ensure that they're stored safely, and to make sure that the labs are set up in the most safe way. Basically, you run around and set up a lab, and you run around and put it away, and you hope that everything gets put back where you want it. And those are the three most dangerous things.

Faced with the dilemma of accepting a policy they oppose or challenging the district, the teachers continue to meet and choose the most appropriate response.

Debriefing the case. This case illustrates an uncomfortable struggle between the district and teachers. The teachers' reflection might even seem rebellious. However, deeper issues surfaced as a result of the teachers' willingness to question the policy and to get organized to have their

voices heard. That they reflected on the issue at all instead of either ig-
noring the policy or abandoning the lab shows the sense of responsibility
with which they took it on.

Did reflection take place? By the definition of reflection used for this
book, certain aspects of the conversation were reflective—particularly because the teachers were using their experience to think about what they
were doing and why. Though they didn't agree with the policy, they were
informed enough to contribute something meaningful back to the
district—far more preferable than the alternatives, which would be to simply ignore the district policy or unquestioningly abandon what they felt
was one of the most successful lessons of the year. However, in order to
make the labs safe—the presumable goal of both groups—would require
one more ingredient between the two parties that unfortunately seemed to
be lacking: an open line of respectful communication and a willingness
to work toward the best and safest chemistry instruction for students.

What supported or hindered reflection? Underwood's case illustrates
the kind of reflection that can take place among a network of colleagues,
which can support reflection in a number of ways. First, colleagues can
share common concerns. Second, they tend to trust one another to hear the
views of their colleagues and to respond with honest opinions. Third, they
work in close proximity, making both impromptu and arranged meetings
possible, even in the course of the school day. These elements supported
reflection.

But Underwood's network was also hindered in its reflection by the situation. Although they could analyze the situation at length and think
ahead for the best outcome for students, they could not *necessarily* take
action on the issue—the most productive outcome of effective reflection.
The decision by the district had been made. Moreover, the teachers were
defending their position—yet another hindrance to reflection. The most
authentic reflection takes place with an attitude of "openness, wholeheartedness, and responsibility" (Dewey, 1933). In this case, the openness
of the teachers to the spirit of the policy *and* of the district to receiving
teacher feedback were both in question.

How was the reflection valuable to teaching? Underwood's network
was combating what they viewed as a nonreflective approach to risk management with a reflective counterargument. The teachers used past experience to seek safer classroom conditions while simultaneously defending

their practice. The balance of safety and engaging instruction is one with which the chemistry teachers routinely dealt. Their willingness to find a suitable balance could only benefit students in the long run.

What can we learn from this case? Underwood's experience with the risk management policy holds an important lesson. The challenges of teaching can be a source of tremendous creative energy that can be applied for better or worse. The teachers used that energy to reflect on experiences with safety matters in the classroom. In the best outcome possible, they and the district would discover a win-win solution, the likes of which can only be gained through collaboration and thoughtful reflection.

SUMMARY

The informal collegial meetings initiated by Nichols and Underwood in this chapter provided opportunities for reflection, even though the potential wasn't always realized. Whether looking back on their practice or deciding what to do and why, they had a safe, collaborative environment in which to reflect. Of all the teachers' reflective experiences, their collegial meetings were some of the more mundane in terms of their direct impact on teaching. Yet all of the teachers expressed general feelings that reflecting with colleagues was worthwhile. Each of the teachers expressed heartfelt appreciation for the groups of which they were a part, lending credence to the assertion that if a serious issue were to arise, these teachers would know where to turn. Unfortunately, significant limits on their time prohibited the teachers from making the most of their reflection more often than not, providing support for an argument developed throughout this book that quality reflection, like quality teaching, takes time.

The next chapter raises a new question about reflection in schools: What is the role of reflection in teacher evaluation? As we shall see, the answer is varied and complex.

Chapter Eight

Teacher Evaluation

What role does reflection play in teacher evaluation? As with the staff, department, and collegial meetings discussed so far, models for evaluating teachers' practice have potential for incorporating reflection. Three systems generally take place:

1. an administrative model, in which administrators evaluate teachers alone;
2. a professional growth model, in which teachers participate in their own evaluation; and
3. a model based on students' responses, in which students evaluate their teachers, usually at a teacher's request.

This chapter views three cases in which teachers are evaluated to determine what role (if any) reflection played in their evaluation. It will show that the teachers actually value evaluation to the extent that it is reflective—they find some experiences to be meaningful, but others downright objectionable.

CASES OF TEACHER EVALUATION

The next case describes King's annual experience with the administrative approach to evaluation, which is so perfunctory it is practically nonexistent.

Case #1: The Administrative System

Once or twice a year as King teaches her class, the administrator designated to evaluate her drops in to observe. He scribbles notes in the back of the room, mostly about what King is doing, then slips out fifteen minutes later. Later that week, he and King sit down and go over the notes. Finding her teaching satisfactory, the administrator presents her with a form that she is to sign, and the ten-minute meeting is over. This is her evaluation for the year.

Debriefing the case. Such a cursory glance at an administrative evaluation of a teacher may seem inconsequential in a book on teachers' reflection. Yet, King's reaction to this situation raises interesting questions about teacher evaluation. The case also provides an informative contrast to other forms of evaluation presented in this chapter. Because all four of the teachers had experienced and commented on this approach to teacher evaluation, their comments are included in the debriefing of the case.

Did reflection take place? As King described this system, it seemed to bear no relationship to reflection, nor was it intended to do so. King and the other teachers viewed the process as not simply nonreflective, but useless, wasteful, and even insulting.

What supported or hindered reflection? As in the staff and department meetings that were designed without reflection in mind, this form of evaluation sorely lacked room for reflection. Why doesn't reflection take place as part of this evaluation system? How could the system be improved to become more reflective and meaningful to teachers? From their perspective, the teachers identified several reasons, discussed below.

One problem that teachers identified with this system was that the classroom observations were rarely complete. In all four teachers' experiences, the classroom observation aspect of the evaluations was not being done at all or not being done well. When administrators deny teachers the kind of useful feedback that can only be garnered from a classroom observation, they close off valuable opportunities for reflection.

The second reason this evaluative system excluded reflection was that even complete classroom observations focused superficially on teacher behavior. King pointed out that in her experience administrators only evaluated the "instructional act," or "in other words, what *you* are *doing.*" She distinguished this from other important aspects of teaching, like the relevance of a particular topic and whether the students were actually learning. In King's opinion, this minimized the value of the process: "You're either satisfactory or unsatisfactory. It doesn't matter what your teaching is like. Unless you're on the road to being dismissed, you're satisfactory." After years of satisfactory teaching, King found little value in this system.

The third and perhaps most definitive reason teacher evaluations typically aren't reflective may be that administrators simply don't have the time to conduct thorough evaluations in this way. Even if the system had potential, King explained, the constraints of the organizational structure would impede a quality debriefing of the observation.

> Administrators don't have time to be a sounding board. . . . We have three administrators and probably ninety people or so on staff. So they have thirty or thirty-five people to sit down and learn their strengths and weaknesses and where they need to be supportive. . . . The scale of the task is just wrong.

The administrative form of evaluation as experienced by the teachers in the study provided few opportunities for reflection, wasn't seen as valuable in most cases, and in some sense seemed structurally impossible.

The classroom observation portion of the system wasn't the only thing lacking. The fourth element of this evaluative system that worked against reflection was that feedback was given through a form. The teachers more often than not resented this form-based approach, finding it especially nonreflective. King summarized the system as she had experienced it: "The principal sits down and talks to me, and I talk back, and then he checks satisfactory, satisfactory, satisfactory, and we both sign it, and it's done." Calling it "superficial," King indicated that this wasn't a very meaningful experience.

To review, the administrative system of evaluating teachers fell short in a number of ways. Reflection was hindered by the quality and content of classroom observations, the amount of time it would take to do them well, and the nature of the forms on which feedback was given. As we've seen, the teachers didn't exactly value the experience.

How was reflection valuable to teaching? Not only did the administrative approach to evaluation not foster reflection; the teachers also unanimously agreed it didn't contribute to their teaching. Citing examples similar to King's case, the teachers asserted that the form-based evaluation method was nonreflective, not meaningful, and sometimes a complete waste of time. The teachers' opinions all seemed congruent with that of King, who described the system as "a singularly unproductive process."

What can we learn from this case? In King's unsatisfactory experience in the case, we can see an unfortunate missed opportunity. If conducted more thoroughly, perhaps such evaluations *could* be both reflective and valuable to teachers. But, in general, to create a reflective experience from this kind of evaluation would be prohibited by the constraints of school size and the scope of an administrator's job. Most likely, this system achieves only its main and most basic goal: to ensure that new teachers are satisfactory and to set in place a system for firing a teacher if necessary. Ideally, these managerial functions would be balanced with the opportunity to support teacher learning.

Fortunately, other ways of evaluating were available in some of the teachers' schools. One that seemed most prevalent focused on teachers' self-guided reflection for professional growth. The discussion turns now to a system designed to encourage professional growth, in the next case from Underwood's school.

Case #2: The Professional Growth System

At the beginning of the school year, Underwood and his colleagues are asked to write down their goals to develop professionally in the coming year. On the given week, he meets with the principal and describes his goals. At the end of the year, he returns for the follow-up meeting to explain how he met the goals. The principal then signs a form and the evaluation is considered complete.

Debriefing the case. In this case, Underwood was invited through the professional growth system to assess his own needs and take steps toward improvement—an approach more amenable to reflection, it would seem, than the administrative system. This system could potentially directly benefit teachers and even students, for a teacher's goals may emerge out of practice of this system. In this case, Underwood's insights about such evaluation experiences are more informative than the actual case and reveal a complex relationship to reflection.

Did reflection take place? At first blush, this system seemed to have reflective potential, provided Underwood actually reflected on his goals. Asked whether or not this system was a learning experience, Underwood responded, "It depends on who you are and how you want to do it. It's wide open for complete B.S.ing. . . . Or, it could be very valuable if you at least took it seriously and you said, okay, I'm going to work on these four things." In other words, whether this approach to evaluation fostered professional growth through reflection was entirely up to him; he saw clearly that he could decide whether or not to reflect on his practice in a way that actually helped him grow.

What supported or hindered reflection? The primary way this system supported reflection was simply by encouraging teachers to think about their goals. But this freedom didn't guarantee reflection. Underwood's own goals illustrate this well.

For this year's goals, Underwood "split the difference" between frivolous and meaningful goals. One goal was something he was already planning to do: participate in the research on reflection informing this book. "I will work with a researcher from the university on teacher reflection, and my hope is that this might help other teachers along the way," wrote Underwood for one of his goals. While this impressed the principal, it wouldn't necessarily enhance Underwood's professional growth. He chuckled, "I was going to do that anyway! So it sounds good, and my principal thought, Wow! That's really neat that you're working with the university! But I had already said I was going to do it." Underwood acknowledged that this goal was inauthentic, even though it met evaluation parameters. In this sense, his evaluation *wasn't* reflective.

His second goal, by contrast, was an authentic goal chosen to guide his own learning. Since a school goal was to increase reading, Underwood made it his goal for professional growth. "Our building goal is to increase reading. So I wanted to work on that. I don't think I would have done it without [the evaluation system], but because of [the system], I put it in, [and] I've taken it seriously." As a result, Underwood decided to have students read a novel in science class. In this sense, his evaluation *was* reflective.

This case illustrates pros and cons of this evaluation system for supporting reflection. Teachers might fail to take advantage of the opportunity to look back and learn from their practice, then set a goal to foster their growth. Or they might think carefully about what to choose as a goal and why—an approach that necessarily involves reflection.

How was reflection valuable to teaching? A significant point in Underwood's case strongly makes the case for reflection. The goal for which he did *not* reflect on his teaching was almost laughable in hindsight, and did little to contribute to his teaching. The goal for which he *did* reflect on his teaching helped him tie student needs and school goals to his instruction. As in many cases throughout this book, experiences involving reflection were more valuable to teachers than those in which reflection was unwelcome. *What can we learn from this case?* Underwood's evaluation was unique among the experience of the teachers in the study. Reflecting on his goals, he saw a link to the broader goals of the school. The benefits served administrative needs for teacher evaluation, while also helping Underwood learn from practice—a benefit for him and potentially his students. But another form of evaluation proved even more valuable, as we see in the next case.

The models of teacher evaluation that the teachers in the study perceived as most beneficial were the ones they designed themselves, in which students gave them feedback on their teaching. These evaluations were neither formal nor required by administrators. Many of the teachers specifically mentioned the advantages of student evaluations and asserted that this model was conducive to their reflection, innovation, and learning. The case below describes Underwood's experience with student evaluations of his teaching.

Case #3: Evaluations from Students

At the end of a fall semester, Underwood finishes teaching microbiology for the first time. To gain perspective on how it went, he asks students to write evaluations of the class. Two main ideas that emerge from their comments get his attention. First, the students want Underwood to find more ways of relating microbiology to the "real world." Reflecting on this response, Underwood remembers the students "really got into the killer diseases." This gets him thinking. "They'd probably really like that book, The Hot Zone. *It's really gory and the students will love that. . . . Plus it's very well researched and scientifically accurate." He sees bringing* The Hot Zone *into the curriculum as a way to respond to the students' request to link science to concrete events.*

Pondering this idea, Underwood also realizes he should temper it in light of another common comment indicating that the class involved too much reading. He thinks,

> *I'm going to try to spend more time making sure they understand the textbook. . . . One of the reading strategies that we've been talking about as a*

school is how to make the higher-level readings accessible. I can do more vo-
cabulary and discussion of topics, and maybe even some in-class reading.

Underwood realizes that this idea can be linked to his professional goal
for evaluation as seen in the previous case: doing more with reading in
his classes. Convinced that these changes will create better learning for
students, and recognizing the worth of the students' needs in light of
school and state goals, he feels inspired to make these changes in his
teaching.

Debriefing the case. This case is one of a large number of examples from
all four of the teachers. Like Underwood, the other teachers often asked students to give them feedback—an activity that helped them continually renew their practice. Ideas for improvement came from the students, as well
as from the teachers' reflections on what the students had to say.

Did reflection take place? Not only was Underwood's case a shining example of reflection as he looked back and learned from his practice; end-of-
term course evaluations by students in general were one of the primary ways
the teachers said they reflected on practice and improved their teaching.

What supported or hindered reflection? Several facets of the student
evaluations made them amenable to reflection. They were self-designed,
allowing Underwood to ask the questions he needed to ask. They were specific to the class, providing context for his reflection. And they were directly related to the next class he would teach, immediately informing his
practice. Underwood could tailor the evaluations to meet his needs.

How was reflection valuable to teaching? All of the teachers used student evaluations as a regular habit of practice. Underwood explicitly emphasized this kind of reflection: "You should [always] have kids reflect
and tell you what they think, and you should take it honestly. If they're all
saying, 'This class sucks,' there's probably good reason." The teachers
saw student evaluations as reflective opportunities and believed they improved teaching and learning.

SUMMARY

In three different approaches to evaluation—the administrative system,
the professional growth system, and evaluation by students—the teachers'

opinions about the effectiveness of evaluations varied greatly. The two kinds of evaluation they found most powerful—evaluation using professional goals and evaluation by students—both involved reflection. The other kind of evaluation—evaluation using an administrative system of "forms"—not only was generally not reflective, but also was perceived as a waste of time. Comparing the cases made it clear that evaluation in the teachers' experiences could be a meaningful opportunity for reflection; unfortunately, it often was not. One more aspect of daily school life revealed a lot about the life of reflection for teachers: the context of teaching. The next chapter will discuss cases from the teachers' classroom practice, for another perspective on reflection in schools.

Chapter Nine

In the Context of Teaching

If reflection seems elusive in the day-to-day events of school life (like meetings and teacher evaluation), then where are the reflective practitioners? The answer: hard at work alone in their classrooms. In dramatic contrast to the largely nonreflective school environments described so far, reflective thought abounded in the context of teaching—not necessarily during structured opportunities, but in what one teacher called reflection "on the fly." These spontaneous learning experiences sprang from inspiration and experimentation before, during, and after classroom instruction.

CASES OF REFLECTION IN THE CONTEXT OF TEACHING

All four teachers told stories of meaningful learning experiences with reflection in the midst of instruction. As King described it, this kind of reflection was "improvisation" that took place in the middle of teaching, often in response to a sudden realization ("This isn't working! Better try something else!"). Nichols called it "being in the moment." This kind of naturally occurring reflection proved to be important to the teachers, providing gains for teachers and students. With slight variations, the process was consistent: teachers would notice a problem, experiment with a solution, see if it worked, and proceed accordingly. We see this sequence of events in an example from Green's experience in the case below.

Case #1: In the Midst of Instruction

Midsemester one fall, it dawns on Green that when she asks students in her algebra class to do an equation, they don't make the effort to get out a piece of paper. Given that the students needed to practice their skills to improve in mathematics, this paper dilemma becomes a puzzle of practice that Green has to figure out.

Once the problem has drawn her attention, she commences a process of experimenting and asking questions. She starts by simply giving students quarter sheets of paper she has retrieved from the recycle bin. She notices that even though the students don't use their own paper, when she gives them paper the students always start to write. She begins keeping a stack of little papers from the recycle bin and handing them out. Reflecting aloud, she says, "They'll do the assignment because that paper's there. That they don't have to wrestle for it, and it's just sitting there, so they might as well write. It's the weirdest thing." Trying to make sense of it, Green wonders, "Why do they do that?" and answers, "It has a lot to do with their background." Reasoning that these students who have had little success in mathematics may have developed the habit of giving up, she decides to be more consistent about prompting them to try. She starts a regular routine of laying paper on each desk before class and putting up a problem. Before she knows it, the students are arriving early, sitting down to that little piece of paper, and working on math! In hindsight, she muses, "It's amazing, the difference it makes." Green's reflective experimentation has led her to solve a puzzle of practice.

Debriefing the case. This example of reflection in the middle of teaching illustrates an experiment that worked, making the reflection valuable to Green and, she believed, to her students. Free to experiment and make changes as needed, she found a solution that made a big difference to these students struggling with mathematics.

Did reflection take place? This case represents a self-described example of reflection—a common example of how all of the teachers regularly experienced reflection. The process is supported by the definition of reflection as learning in the midst of practice to make informed decisions about what to do, when to do it, and why.

What supported or hindered reflection? Unlike the structured activities prompted by administrators in Underwood's grant-preparation staff meeting, for example, or in King's department meeting to align teaching goals with school standards, Green's reflection in this case was an unstructured process, a natural outgrowth of teaching. Yet, it was supported by several subtle factors. First, it was sparked by a challenging situation and the realization that students weren't learning—a common motivator mentioned by all of the teachers. Second, it relied on Green's expertise as a teacher, as she drew on her insider's knowledge of her students. Third, it suited an iterative process of teaching, in which teachers can experiment in their classes and see the results of their efforts. Unlike with activities that failed to foster reflection, the purpose was concrete and clearly important.

But *not* free to change the school schedule accordingly, Green also found her solution didn't last. She needed time between classes to set up the room with the papers, and it wasn't long before this time was infringed upon by another teacher's class, which was suddenly assigned to share the room. Green reported, "Our school is getting so crowded that it's very rare to have your whole room to yourself." Although Green's freedom in her classroom supported her reflection, the overcrowded conditions of the school hampered her ability to sustain the change it implied.

How was the reflection valuable to teaching? Despite a change in circumstances that made her strategy to help the algebra students harder to implement, Green knew that other situations would arise in which reflection would again improve learning. She pointed out that reflection was an ongoing process and that different classes would need different strategies all the time. "[So] you keep trying little things . . . and you have to keep altering what you did. Even though it was a good strategy, it's not going to work for every group of kids. . . . You think about those things as you teach." Green saw learning in the midst of instruction as a reflective, valuable, ongoing process.

What can we learn from this case? Perhaps the most significant contribution of this case as an example of reflection in daily school life is that teachers reflect all the time as part of their practice. Green's success with this one small group of students is one of dozens of experiences described by the four accomplished teachers, suggesting that reflection should be honored as a regular part of quality teaching.

But such reflection didn't take place only in the classroom. By far the most prolific kind of reflection these teachers experienced, reflection in the form of private thought and conversation, took place between classes and after school. When they were not actually teaching a class, the teachers were able to take a little more time to think things over. Nichols said succinctly what all of the teachers seemed to believe about this kind of reflection: "Reflection is very important, because when we look back on what it is that we've done, we see it a little differently. We give it time and space." In casual conversations with colleagues, in reviewing the day's events, or in assessing student learning, these instances took place on a daily basis. As opposed to more formal collegial meetings on issues, these conversations emerged gradually from interactions throughout the day that were reflective, valuable, or both. An example came from an impromptu conversation between Underwood and a colleague, seen in the next case.

Case #2: Between Classes and After School

Underwood and another chemistry teacher in the department—good friends and close colleagues—usually eat lunch together. Given their similar teaching situations, the conversation often turns to chemistry. One day, they hit upon an issue on which they both want to improve. After teaching organic chemistry for five years, they suddenly realize they have always had the same complaint—that the class is too "reading oriented" and all the "cool labs" are at the end. Out of time, they agree to regroup at the end of the day.

After school, they continue their conversation. They discuss the sequence of the syllabus and agree that students need the content at the beginning of the course to understand the labs at the end. They also agree that the class feels unbalanced as a result. Putting their heads together, they try to find a way to change around the curriculum for a more satisfactory course. Thinking creatively, Underwood and his colleague soon discover that one of the labs can be used for a different concept altogether. They decide to make the change and see how it impacts the class.

The following semester, Underwood tries out this new idea. His satisfaction with the results is obvious: "We just took this whole week and moved it up to the beginning, and loved it. It was a great idea. . . . The students really enjoyed it." For reasons like this, he calls the chance to reflect with his colleagues "invaluable."

Debriefing the case. Underwood's experience here captures a type of experience described by all four of the teachers. Spontaneous conversations between colleagues frequently erupted into creative thought and action borne out of collegial reflection. But the effectiveness of such conversations varied, as described in the discussion below.

Did reflection take place? This case fits the definition of reflection and illustrates a key aspect of it. Underwood and his colleague embody the mindset of openness, wholeheartedness, and responsibility when they voluntarily seek a new way of teaching, consider the alternatives, and commit to teaching the best class they can.

What supported or hindered reflection? The most obvious assets to Underwood were the collegial relationship and the time that made such conversations possible in the day. When present, these supported reflection. When they were absent, the process was hindered.

Underwood specifically highlighted the importance of good collegial relationships to collaborative reflection. He saw himself as being in a good situation with his colleagues, who all got along and felt comfortable reflecting together. Underwood said that made it possible for them to carry on a dialogue: "'Hey, how'd that lab work for you?' 'It didn't.' 'Why not?' And we talk about it." But Underwood also said he knew of departments at his school in which the teachers didn't talk. "That's actually common," he claimed, suggesting that such reflective conversations may not be the norm.

Expressing his appreciation for midday reflection, Underwood also noted that the time he valued so much depended on a set of circumstances he felt were unusual. Teachers at his school had a fifty-minute lunch period—a length of time fortuitously created by a schedule accommodating overcrowding. He explained: "We had so many kids that we needed to free up space for whole periods. Lunch is designed to cover an entire class period, which frees up that many rooms, so we can fit 1,900 people into a building built for 1,4[00]." The system worked for the students' schedules and serendipitously worked for the teachers, too. In Underwood's words, "You can sit and talk and reflect and get some stuff done right in the middle of the day." But with new discussions about changes in the schedule, the fifty-minute lunch was being threatened. "I worry, because we're looking at new schedules," Underwood reported, implying that those new schedules may shorten lunch—and shrink his opportunity to reflect with colleagues even more.

How was the reflection valuable to teaching? In Underwood's own words, the reflection in this case was "invaluable." The ultimate results of the case improved his instruction and, according to his students, improved the chemistry class. This pattern was true for all of the teachers when conversations with their colleagues turned to reflection and continuous improvement of their practice—an element of quality teaching.

What can we learn from this case? This case illustrates many aspects of midday reflection experienced by all of the teachers. As a result of their collaborative reflection, the teachers frequently achieved results for their teaching, classes, and students.

However, a closer look at the realities of schools revealed that such conversations were jeopardized daily. Reflective and valuable though they might be, they were also rather brief, taking place for ten or fifteen minutes here and there—segments of time that fit into teachers' rare free spaces in the day.

Naturally, not every free moment was reflective—teachers did, after all, have to eat, talk to students, go to meetings, and plan for afternoon classes when they weren't actively engaged in instruction. The teachers also spent plenty of time with their colleagues talking of nothing more exciting than the weather. Conversations between colleagues, more often than not, were simply social conversations. But when conditions were right, the teachers appreciated the chance to reflect with their colleagues.

And yet, as seen in the next case, the informal existence of reflection fell short of perfect. Even though teachers viewed daily reflection as a staple of teaching, it could also be seriously unreliable. The teachers could only reflect on the things that they saw, heard, and remembered. On one hand, this was an obvious and avoidable reality of everyday instruction. On the other hand, it highlighted the isolation of teachers and the problems that slipped by unnoticed in the absence of strategies to help teachers "see" their own practice. Examples of such strategies are found later in this book. Here we view one case in which a teacher, with the aid of another perspective on his teaching, was able to reflect on an issue that he otherwise would have missed.

Case #3: Over Time with a Puzzle of Practice

Previewing a lesson he is about to teach for a classroom observer, Underwood states a glaring contradiction. The lesson will begin with a lecture on the concept of mass ratio. Then, he will give a demonstration

*to "spice up" the lesson. Underwood adds oddly, "The demonstration
really doesn't have anything to do with mass ratio, but it's meaningful,
and they can start to put a tie to their daily lives." Underwood wonders
aloud whether other science teachers would think teaching mass ratio
was important, but says, regardless, he always teaches it. In the next
class, he teaches the lesson as planned. The students are
indeed engaged, but any connection between the demonstration and
mass ratio is missing. Instead, the lab activity simply serves to break up
the lecture.*

*Later, Underwood reads a summary of the lesson, written by the class-
room observer. He reads aloud: "I wonder how the demonstration relates
to the idea of mass ratio." To himself, he says, "I'm sure some of the kids
were wondering that, too!"*

*Asked to comment, Underwood expresses a nagging concern that the
lesson might not be worth doing. He imagines there are other ways
the students could come to understand mass ratio and comes up with some
ideas midstream. He considers using the demonstration for other concepts, like balancing equations, heat transfer, and kinetic molecular
theory. He ultimately realizes he is using a "good lab" for a fairly minor
concept and decides to change the lesson to resolve the contradiction.*

Debriefing the case. The preceding case reveals an important idea
about teachers' reflection, particularly when it involves what they do in
their classrooms: teachers must first recognize and identify an issue before they can reflect on it. Only when Underwood detected the contradiction in his lesson did it seem possible for him to make changes in
practice—he only identified the contradiction with the aid of an observer's perspective.

Did reflection take place? Over time, Underwood was able to see a
problem with his own reasoning in setting up this lesson. With prompting,
he reflected on what he'd done. He chose to examine the contradiction between the lesson content and the demonstration, and he took steps to improve his teaching based on what he learned.

What supported or hindered reflection? This case is included to reveal
the importance of objective perspective—a mechanism by which teachers
can study their practice. Even though on some level Underwood was
aware of the contradictions inherent in the lesson, he didn't consciously
address the problem until prompted by someone else.

The technique in this case supported Underwood's reflection: by reading an observer's summary of his class and pondering a question asked by that observer, he was able to move into a more inquiring frame of mind and see his lesson in a new way. Without such a structure, the oddity in Underwood's lesson might have gone unnoticed for years. Certainly teachers do recognize puzzles of practice on their own, as seen in Green's case with her algebra class earlier in this chapter. Underwood's case simply shows that teachers are as likely to overlook challenges as they are to spot them.

How was reflection valuable to teaching? Assuming Underwood actually made the changes he described at the end of the case, reflection would have impacted his teaching. He would have created a more congruous lesson, one in which a minor concept was treated as such and the demonstration held content-based meaning for students. This awareness motivated Underwood to change this lesson.

From this perspective, Underwood's reflection may have added value to his teaching. Interestingly, however, his evolving discovery that his pedagogy didn't match this lesson's content barely seemed conscious. This illustrates an aspect of reflection: whereas it can prompt "Aha!" reactions, at other times it may pass by barely noticed.

What can we learn from this case? This case emphasizes the importance of teachers taking time to consciously reflect on lessons over time, with the help of a second perspective when possible. Doing so may help them analyze teaching strategies that would otherwise go unnoticed— whether they're effective or not.

SUMMARY

Reflection in the context of teaching involved a complex assortment of activities. The teachers reflected alone and with others in the midst of instruction, between classes, after school, and over time. Although the value of their experiences also varied, overall the teachers agreed: reflecting in, on, and for practice was an important part of teaching.

But constraints of the school context made it difficult to reflect. Even as reflection sprinkled the teachers' days, an equally limitless number of missed opportunities slipped by unnoticed. In part, these missed opportunities grew out of an understandable limitation of perspective, but in part, the teachers also blamed the limitations on the conditions of teaching—the constraints of time and the difficulty of observing practice that has become automatic. The next chapter reviews in more detail themes in the teachers' reflection in the contexts of schools and how those contexts influence the effectiveness of reflection.

Chapter Ten

Reflection and the Conditions of Schools

A REVIEW OF THIS SECTION: REFLECTION AND THE CONDITIONS OF SCHOOLS

The previous sections illustrated diverse activities and opportunities that arose in the daily lives of four accomplished teachers. In staff and department meetings, informal collegial meetings, teacher evaluation, and the contexts of teaching, the teachers experienced both reflective and nonreflective activities, with mixed results for their teaching. Their experiences revealed that reflection *could* take place anytime, anywhere. But the reflection that these activities permitted for addressing the issues was too abstract, too forced, or too rushed.

This chapter discusses themes from the cases in this section on reflection in schools—the professional context. The first section of the chapter discusses the place in schools for reflection, an item often last on the priority list. It also discusses challenges of school-based reflection. The second section of this chapter summarizes the lessons learned from the cases, as well as the advantages and disadvantages of reflection in schools. Overall, we can conclude that school-based activities in general have an unrealized potential for supporting reflection.

The Place of Reflection in Teaching

A disturbing pattern can be seen as we look across the cases that calls into question the viability of reflection in schools. The cases are deceiving; they suggest that the teachers reflected far more often than they actually did.

Although the teachers were certainly seen reflecting in their practice, they were quick to point out that they rarely had time for reflection on a regular basis. Their busy schedules made reflection last on a long list of priorities, despite the value they placed on reflection in teaching. This chapter explores the teachers' views on this reality and its impact on their reflection.

The Last Item on the Priority List

Despite examples of reflection in their teaching, all four of the teachers agreed that reflection was rarely a priority. Underwood gave this description of a day in the life of a teacher:

> There [are] so many hours in the day. So, if you're a teacher, every day you make these choices. So your choices are, well, I'm done with my eight hours, and now I can correct these papers for the next two hours, or I can spend the next two hours setting up this really cool lab, or I can spend the next two hours helping [a student who's] behind, or I can spend the next two hours calling ten different parents. [He sighs] Or, I could go home and spend time with my fiancée.

Then, almost as an afterthought, he added one more choice: "or you can reflect." Despite its importance, reflection showed up last in a long list of other pressing matters.

Reflection and the Busyness of Teaching

The incredible busyness of teaching suggested it would be important to schedule reflection into the regular teaching day. But again, the teachers agreed, this was almost never done. Three of the four teachers' comments on this subject echo each other hauntingly:

Underwood: There's really not a lot of reflection built into teaching in general.

Green: There's no time built into a teacher's day to reflect.

King: There's no time structured in a teacher's day for reflection. Schools and departments have never been used that way.

Each of these three teachers expressed a belief that reflection was not structured into their lives in the school context.

The Invisibility of Ongoing Reflection

Rounding out the picture a bit, however, was a comment by Nichols. She believed that even when it was not structured in, reflection did still take place. She said, "A lot of my reflection's in my head. . . . I bet you teachers would be just shocked at how often they are . . . reflecting." Thus, Nichols implied that reflection happened subconsciously, whether time was set aside for it or not. Nevertheless, another comment from King suggested that to introduce reflection into teaching would be a change: "There's very little chance to reflect in teaching. It's not something that's structured into a teacher's day or week or month." The teachers all indicated that reflection was not a formally recognized part of their jobs.

The Absence of Reflection in Schools

That schools weren't structured for reflection didn't mean it couldn't be encouraged in less formal ways; unfortunately, the teachers indicated that it wasn't. Talking about how often teachers were encouraged to reflect on their practice, King said it was "hit or miss . . . and it's mostly miss." Green's experience was even more discouraging: "In education, in all the years I've been in it, I don't think I've ever really been asked to reflect on what I do." In other words, the habits of reflection evidenced by these four teachers spoke more to their own initiatives than to the context of their schools.

When Reflection Actually Takes Place

Since little time was available to reflect in the course of the day, the teachers found other ways to attend to the issues. Each described a different approach. For Underwood, reflection was "minutes here and minutes there." For King, it was "a continuous meditation . . . going on just below the surface of the mind. For Nichols, it was "kind of just in my head all of a sudden." Nichols supposed teachers were reflecting much more than they knew, suggesting one more hidden element of reflection: it may or may not be a process of which teachers are aware.

The Challenges of Reflecting in School

Again looking across the cases of school-based reflection reveals another troubling pattern: not one of the teachers' experiences was ideal for supporting reflection—a reality that warrants consideration. Here, challenges of school-based reflection, focusing squarely on the conditions of schools that work against reflection and, consequently, quality teaching, are discussed.

The Risk of Reflecting

One challenge of reflection involved professional risk. "Truly reflective practice means you also have to be vulnerable," said Green. Green's case of the algebra students who wouldn't do assignments without a piece of paper, Underwood's case of the demonstration that didn't enhance the content of a lesson, and King's case of the students who were lacking in note-taking skills all required an admission on the part of the teachers that something wasn't working in their teaching. Not all teachers are willing to take the public risk that professional reflection entails.

The Isolation of Teaching

Another challenge facing reflection, as King explained, involved the isolated nature of teaching.

> Another reason we don't reflect very much in this profession other than what one might be naturally inclined to do is that there's almost no one to reflect to. Who does a teacher talk with during the day? The kids. Well, you know, in terms of reflecting on teaching practice, they can give you information, how things work, what they like and what they don't like, but they don't have the perspective to be very reflective about teaching.

Teachers have little opportunity for collegial contact in the egg-crate structure of schools.

Supporting Reflection in Schools

The challenges discussed above indicate a need for structured activity to support and encourage reflection. The teachers agreed. "If you want physical, hard evidence of reflection, you have to provide time to do it. If you want [teachers] to verbalize their reflection, you have to give them time to do that," reported Green. She continued by pointing out if time *were* made available for teachers to reflect on their practice, the experience would have to be meaningful. As was illustrated in many instances in this chapter, the teachers resented having to "sit down and reflect for reflection's sake." In that kind of reflection, Green stated emphatically, "There's no benefit. The time that I have is too valuable to do that."

Meaningful reflection, the teachers asserted, was vital to quality teaching. Unfortunately, they also agreed it was a challenge to create, much less sustain, opportunities to habitually reflect on their practice in significant ways. As a result, even teachers who saw themselves as reflective were more typically constrained to minimally reflective ways of teaching. As Underwood said, "You just fly by the seat of your pants."

LESSONS LEARNED ABOUT REFLECTION IN SCHOOLS

In the school context, many if not most of the activities had potential to support and encourage reflection. However, that potential wasn't always realized, with the exception of teachers' private reflection. We can learn about reflection in schools by analyzing the situations in which reflection was both present and valuable compared with those in which it was not. The discussion below compares and contrasts the cases for an overall view of the effectiveness of reflection in schools.

The Importance of Teacher Involvement

The cases of reflection that the teachers most valued—those that were both reflective *and* valuable—most often included activities designed and initiated by teachers, not administrators or programs. Experiences in this category included conversations with colleagues, student evaluations, impromptu experimentation in the middle of class, and time spent looking back at the end of the day. Few of these stood out as being highly valuable, but they counted in the teachers' minds as being at least worthwhile uses of their time. In those reflective experiences that the teachers did find highly valuable, they embraced the opportunity to reflect in private, initiating their own conversations, experiments, and thoughts.

The Value of Conscientious Inquiry

Across the school context, the most valuable examples of reflection emerged from teachers' stories of conscientious inquiry into the learning of their students, like Underwood's analysis of his microbiology and organic chemistry classes. Such efforts revealed the initiative and persistence of the teachers, who seemed willing to work out the puzzles of practice to improve their students' learning. However, numerous contradictions remained unaddressed, as when Underwood disregarded the content focus and chose a demonstration that didn't further learning.

The Scarcity of Valuable Reflection

Despite the impossibility of reflecting on all of the matters that arose, the teachers found reflection that did occur to be valuable. When the teachers gave their reflective attention to critical matters of teaching and learning, they saw new ways to support student success in school. Unfortunately, the teachers asserted unanimously that the time for reflection was scarce.

Resistance to Nonreflective Activities

In sharp contrast to the teachers' reflective response to the events in their classrooms and the needs of their students, their apathetic, if not outwardly resistant, attitude toward the nonreflective activities imposed on them was striking. Staff meetings, department meetings, and the administrative evaluation system may have served some purpose to administration, but the import was generally lost on the teachers, who saw these activities as a waste of their time. Reflection was perceived as uninvited if not unwelcome. The teachers expressed frustration and bitterness at having to spend time on agendas that they felt had little relevance to their teaching and at not having the time or the encouragement to focus on their own needs as teachers. The issues that the teachers were dealing with wheedled their way into the conversation during these organized activities—signaling the need for reflection—but were usually dismissed unless a teacher managed to force the issue.

In a profession widely recognized for its struggles with time, the allocation of this valuable resource for such activities seemed wasteful. Particularly striking is that most of the activities in this category were organized by administrators without the teachers' input or interest. This evidenced a disconnection between what teachers felt they needed to do and how they were actually required to spend their time. Overall, the teachers' opinion about reflection in schools was that it was highly valued in theory, but seldom supported in practice.

The Benefit of Nonreflective Activities

Not all of the nonreflective activities seen in the cases evoked teachers' resistance. In fact, they actually appreciated the chance to talk without having to reflect. One characteristic example in this group was Nichols's lunchtime study group, which was interesting because it showed one teacher's attempt to help fellow teachers reflect—an attempt that didn't quite succeed. Although the teachers valued the time together, they lacked the kind of structured activity that could push conversation into reflection. What they did have was a cohesive collegial group—a foundation upon which reflection could take place, as we'll see in later cases in this book.

The Ineffectiveness of Forced Reflection

Importantly, the existence of reflection didn't guarantee any activity's success. Special project staff and department meetings, as well as the professional growth model of teacher evaluation, were designed to be reflective but were viewed as unsuccessful and not meaningful by the teachers. Using staff and department time for quality reflection would have required more than the principals' initial efforts to design reflection into an activity, like attention to the needs of the teachers and the connection of the activity to teachers' classroom-based concerns.

From examining reflection in schools, we can see that supporting reflection is a complicated endeavor. To make sense of this complex environment and its impact on reflection, the advantages and disadvantages of reflecting in schools will now be considered.

Advantages of Reflection in the Professional Context

The advantages of reflecting in the school context as suggested by these four teachers boil down to one element: location.

The fact that the teachers could reflect with their students, with their colleagues, and in the building in which they spent their working days was a significant advantage, given the proximity of people and resources with which and upon which they could reflect. Certain elements of the location, such as the norms of the culture, made the school a less-than-ideal context for reflection, but nevertheless, it had tremendous potential given the number of matters for reflection that arose on a day-to-day basis.

Beyond the potential afforded by location, little else in this context seemed to support reflection. Instead, the other elements that made the reflection possible in this context arose primarily from the teachers' individual personalities, situations, and motivation—individualized characteristics not attributable to school contexts in general.

Disadvantages of Reflection in the Professional Context

The disadvantages were more numerous in this context than the advantages. The disadvantages included three items: time for reflection, structure and activities, and culture.

Time for reflection. According to all four of the teachers in this study, time simply wasn't made available for teachers to reflect as part of their practice. With the exception of administratively organized activities that the teachers often dismissed or resented, reflection occurred only when the teachers made the time or took the time to do so.

Structure and activities. Despite evidence of teachers being reflective, it often seemed that what counted as reflection by the teachers' definitions and the definition presented earlier in this book barely skimmed the surface. The materials, questions, guidelines, and directions needed to guide teachers from conversation to deeper, more meaningful reflection were largely absent. As a result, potentially reflective opportunities were lost, even when teachers seemed to be seeking ways to reflect on critical issues of teaching. A more structured activity such as those found in other contexts—as we shall see in the next section—or at least the skills to ask and address helpful questions, might have avoided situations in which teachers left potentially reflective conversations feeling frustrated, dissatisfied, or helpless.

Culture. More than once for each teacher, it was evident that negative feelings and a lack of community or a culture of trust characterized the school environment. Given the significance of these elements as commonly cited requirements for reflection, such a culture persistently worked against reflection.

Looking at the advantages and disadvantages of this context has shed light on what might be needed to support reflection in schools. In the next two sections of this book, we will be able to compare these findings with advantages and disadvantages in other contexts—in programs for professional development and on teachers' personal time.

SUMMARY

Having discussed the place of reflection in schools, the challenge of reflection therein, and the advantages and disadvantages of reflection in this context, this section closes with a rather discouraging picture. That the schools were ineffective in supporting reflection is hardly surprising. Schools are notorious for bureaucratic structures (Sarason, 1996) and teachers for being "prisoners of time" (Kane, 1994). One wonders what would happen if reflection were supported in a way that was meaningful to teachers, giving them the time, tools, and motivation to look back on and learn from their practice. In fact, such structures have been created in certain programs. In particular, programs for assessment and professional development have emerged that purposefully target reflection as a goal for teacher learning. Although the prevalence of such activities seemed limited or at least hidden in the school context, Nichols, Green, King, and Underwood each had indeed been involved in professional programs—experiences that they voluntarily took part in on top of their day-to-day jobs of teaching. How did their experiences with reflection differ when they were embedded in these inherently reflective programs? That question is the subject of the next section of the book. The next section moves from discussing the complex reality of the school as a context for reflection to a more successful context—one in which teachers do address different issues in a strategy of mind over matter.

Chapter Eleven

Reflecting in Programs: The Programmatic Context

Teaching is an intellectual activity (Shulman, 1987). As researchers opposed to a technician model of teaching assert, reflective practitioners do not mechanically manage the topics of teaching. Rather, they apply their *minds* to these matters, using conscientious, ever-changing strategies well suited to the complexity of classroom life.

Such intellectual awareness can be challenging, and some have said it comes only with experience (Berliner, 1988; Grossman, 1989; Jay, 2001). But programs of teacher assessment are sprouting up across the nation with the intention to guide teachers in stretching their thinking about teaching so that they can become more thoughtful about what they do and why. This section shifts the focus from daily school life to programs specifically designed to foster reflection. This is called the "programmatic context," because such programs become settings of their own, typically taking place outside the regular teaching day. Such programs involve the completion of particular, well-defined tasks and command a more focused, structured kind of reflection than does the school context.

Nichols, Green, King, and Underwood all took part in such programs. Again, cases include both successful and unsuccessful outcomes, providing us with insights regarding their advantages and limitations. What happens when teachers engage in activities designed to be reflective? Does reflection actually occur as planned? Does teachers' reflection become more consistent or more meaningful? This section examines the benefits and drawbacks of reflecting as part of a program.

Each chapter in this section highlights one or more of the teachers' experiences in a particular program. This chapter includes an organizing framework for understanding teachers' experiences as well as their general perspectives on program-based reflection. Subsequent chapters present specific cases from the teachers' participation in programs of teacher assessment: the National Board for Professional Teaching Standards certification process, a voluntary district program for teacher assessment, and mentoring programs. The final chapter in this section discusses themes across the cases from the teachers' experiences with reflection in programs.

A FRAMEWORK FOR LEARNING FROM THE CASES

When studying reflection in the teachers' daily school lives, earlier chapters used a framework for differentiating between widely varying experiences in which reflection was either planned or precluded, present or not present, and meaningful or not meaningful to teachers. To do so, three central questions were used to debrief each case:

1. Did reflection take place?
2. What supported or hindered reflection?
3. How was reflection valuable to teaching?

Key lessons from each case were also summarized in response to a fourth question: What can we learn from this case? These questions will be used to make sense of the teachers' experiences reflecting as part of the programs for professional growth.

However, as we shall see, reflecting in the contexts of programs differs markedly from reflecting in the contexts of schools. Elements of the programs complicate our ability to determine how reflection is supported and encouraged. Two particular issues arise in program-based reflection: first, a tension between reflection and other purposes of the programs and second, a tension between teachers' expertise and the level of expertise aimed at by the programs. These will be discussed in brief here.

Reflection as One of Many Goals

All of the programs seen in the upcoming chapters serve multiple purposes: they aim to both *assess* teaching and to *encourage professional growth.* This introduces a number of tensions. First, teachers may be required to reflect on their practice even when no challenge has presented itself. Second, teachers must perform organizational tasks like paperwork and editing that may overshadow their reflection. Third, although reflection may be beneficial, the pressures of evaluation, such as the need to receive high marks, may take precedence over improving one's practice. These tensions, widely recognized in discussions of reflective assessment (Ingvarson, 1998), should be kept in mind.

A One-Size-Fits-All Model of Reflection

All of the programs in this section necessarily entail consistent requirements. Out of fairness and practicality, they provide opportunities for all eligible teachers to participate. Within certain parameters, assessments must be constant, regardless of teachers' job circumstances, years of experience, or skill. This raises a question about whether all teachers are likely to find the experiences equally meaningful. Will a teacher with twenty years' experience be as challenged by a program as one with only five? Will a teacher known for subject matter expertise find it easier to succeed than one known for fostering community among students? In some ways, this is a more critical question than whether or how reflection takes place in the programs, for even the most carefully crafted activities have the potential to be ineffectual when they don't challenge teachers to learn.

The two issues discussed above surface periodically in the teachers' experiences with reflection described in this section. As appropriate, comments about these issues will be noted to point out the challenges occurring when reflection is embedded in programs.

THE NATURE OF REFLECTION
IN THE CONTEXT OF PROGRAMS

Before reflection in the three different programs experienced by the four teachers can be explored, some general comments about reflection in these contexts can be helpful. Let us now examine some themes found across the programs—as well as significant differences between the programs—that will inform our understanding of the cases presented later. (*Note*: Because all of the teachers participated in the National Board certification process, while only one or two participated in the other programs, the discussion in this section heavily emphasizes this program.)

An Expanded Definition of Reflection

The four teachers' perspectives on reflection in general were presented in chapter 4. Their opinions were consistent with the definition of reflection used in this book. Here, modifications of the definition that accompanied the programs are considered.

New Ideas about Reflection from the Programs

Whereas the definition of reflection in this book has emphasized learning from experience to improve teaching practice, the programs highlighted the need for such reflection to be systematic and to incorporate alternative perspectives—elements that made reflection more rigorous.

We can see these added elements by looking at how two of the featured programs define reflection. The National Board asserts that accomplished teachers *must* "think systematically about their practice and learn from experience" (National Board for Professional Teaching Standards, 2001). Without using the word "reflection," the National Board captures the essence of the concept, along with an implication that to reflect requires a systematic approach. A voluntary, district-organized program for teacher evaluation using Danielson's *Enhancing Professional Practice* (1996) also describes reflection as congruent with the definition this book has used:

> The ability to reflect on teaching is the mark of a true professional. Through reflection, real growth and therefore excellence are possible. By trying to understand the consequences of actions and by contemplating alternative courses of action, teachers expand their repertoire of practice. (p. 106)

This definition, too, shows reflection to be a core part of the program and implies that reflection ultimately results in excellence. These definitions of reflection used by the programs expand the definition of reflection used in this book to include other assumptions, that reflection is expected to be "systematic" and related to "growth" and "excellence."

New Ideas about Reflection from the Teachers

It wasn't just the programs that presented expanded views of reflection. The teachers themselves described an expanded definition of reflection when they talked about it in the context of programs. An interesting contrast surfaced when the teachers described program-based reflection compared with their thoughts about reflection in the contexts of schools: whereas their independent, self-directed reflection was based on their own personal standards, their reflection in the context of different programs was based on an external standard.

Underwood found that the external standard showed him a very different picture of his teaching. He said, "You read the standards and you realize that what you thought was your best [lesson] isn't!" He contrasted this with the internal standard that usually accompanied his reflection. "What oftentimes I consider the 'best' [lesson] is what the kids enjoyed the most. I just assumed that that was the one that they were learning the most from." Looking at the external standards, he discovered his assumption to be wrong.

> You look at [the lesson again], and . . . you go, "Oh! You know, [the students] really didn't learn a lot out of it," or "It really wasn't all that in-depth. They really enjoyed doing it . . . but they didn't learn a lot." Then you think, if I'm going to use this [lesson] in [my National Board] portfolio, then maybe I need to improve it.

Underwood's description revealed that the definition of reflection operating in the program implied some accountability not typically present in school-based reflection.

Comparing their practice with an external standard involved answering questions about practice—something less frequently found in teachers' independent reflection. As Underwood said, "We always think about what we've done, but you don't tend to ask yourself specific questions." The experiences of the teachers in this section revealed that an external standard made them consider questions they otherwise would not have.

An Added Purpose for Reflecting on Practice

Compared with the reasons the teachers gave for reflecting in the context of their daily work, their reasons for reflecting in the contexts of different programs were characterized by a more prudent purpose. That is, their reflection served an additional goal—for instance, to get certified by the National Board. The teachers explained how reflection helped them meet their goals for the programs:

Underwood: You reflect on what you've done in the past to try to relate it to what's going to go into the portfolios.

Green: If you don't reflect on your teaching, you can't be certified.

King: Many of the entries are specifically reflective, so you have to reflect, or else you couldn't complete the entry.

Nichols: Reflection is the "what you've learned" part of the portfolio.

In their opinions, reflection served the purpose of meeting the goals of the program and the related purpose of changing practice as needed in order to meet those goals.

That the teachers were reflecting for the purpose of particular programs didn't mean the experiences weren't valuable. Their comments suggested the opposite. They valued reflection highly as a contribution to their teaching, regardless of what initiated the process. Nevertheless, they also realized that the stakes were higher when they reflected for assessment purposes. Describing the National Board process, King said, "Reflection happens for your own benefit or the benefit of yourself and your students. [But in the National Board process], it was actually for the benefit of your audience. We would be evaluated." A constant awareness that reflection was important for their success in a program was a theme throughout the teachers' experiences in this section.

SUMMARY

To review, this section of the book features cases of the teachers' experiences with reflection in the context of particular programs of teacher assessment, each of which was designed to foster reflection: the National Board for Professional Teaching Standards certification process, a voluntary district program for teacher assessment, and mentoring programs.

This section will again be asking questions about each case, keeping in mind the multiple goals inherent in such programs. We can expect to see teachers depending on a definition of reflection that emphasizes systematic thinking about practice and improved teaching excellence. We can also expect to see teachers focusing more on external standards as they assess their own practice and strive to meet the goals of the programs. The discussion starts now with the first set of cases drawn from the teachers' experiences with the National Board for Professional Teaching Standards.

Chapter Twelve

The NBPTS Certification Process

Is an accomplished teacher by definition a reflective teacher? According to the National Board for Professional Teaching Standards (NBPTS, or "National Board"), the answer is yes. As any teacher familiar with the National Board can attest, certification by the board requires a rigorous process of proving one's teaching to be accomplished by meeting a number of high standards of teaching (Jenkins, 2000; Swain, 1999; Mahaley, 1999). It is also a process believed to activate in-depth reflection (Darling-Hammond, 1998; Jay, 2001). Yet for all the board's acclaim, the value of certification in terms of reflection can vary from teacher to teacher. Before witnessing this in the cases, it seems important to summarize the certification process itself, for National Board certification involves a very specific set of activities that have bearing on our discussion of reflection.

The NBPTS sets standards for teaching and recognizes teachers who meet them. As part of its mission, the National Board aims to recognize accomplished teaching. Certification is a symbol of achievement that carries some measure of status. The mission of the National Board is

> to establish high and rigorous standards for what accomplished teachers should know and be able to do, to develop and operate a national, voluntary system to assess and certify teachers who meet these standards and to advance related education reforms for the purpose of improving student learning in American schools. (National Board for Professional Teaching Standards, 2001)

The process of becoming certified explicitly calls for reflection as teachers compare their practice with the standards and prepare materials to prove that they have met them.

Nichols, Green, King, and Underwood are all National Board–certified teachers. To achieve certification—a professional honor that can carry financial benefits—they were required to complete a test and create portfolios of practice. The National Board provided an extensive set of materials for candidates going through the process, including extensive descriptions of standards for teaching, as well as guidelines, suggestions, directions, questions, and requirements for completing portfolio entries.

The portfolios the teachers created contained six entries, which varied according to the subject matter and level at which each teacher taught. (Underwood's portfolio addressed areas in teaching adolescent/young adult science, Green's in adolescent/young adult mathematics, King's in adolescent/young adult social studies/history, and Nichols's in adolescent/young adult English and language arts.) Entries required teachers to highlight aspects of practice, such as real-life application of knowledge, assessment of student understanding, and classroom discussion. The portfolio-building process involved different activities, such as examining videotapes of teaching, analyzing student work, and reflecting on standards—all of which provided opportunities for the teachers to reflect on their practice.

Summarizing the entire process, Underwood stated that the "National [Board] certification process is one big reflection on what you do." The other teachers agreed. And yet, the degree to which the teachers found reflection in the certification process to be meaningful varied by activity and by teacher. They found the process alternatingly motivational and frustrating, implying that although the process may be both reflective and powerful, it may not be consistently so. We see this illustrated in the cases that follow of the teachers' experiences with reflection and the National Board.

CASES FROM THE NBPTS CERTIFICATION PROCESS

This chapter introduces teachers' experiences with different aspects of the portfolio process. Unquestionably, each case involved reflection. In some cases, the result had a profound effect on teaching. In other cases, however, the impact seemed negligible, despite enormous effort and frustration. In all of the cases, the teachers acknowledged that the significant benefits they derived from the National Board process came at a price.

The first case illustrates one of the most successful experiences any of the teachers had with the National Board. In this case, Underwood spotted a disconnection between the accomplished teaching expected by the National Board and his actual teaching in the classroom. A process of reflection ensued and he revised his lesson to improve student learning. By the time his lesson was ready for inclusion in his National Board portfolio, he felt confident his lesson was strong.

Case #1: Creating a Videotape of Practice

As part of his National Board portfolio, Underwood is required to videotape and analyze a lesson in which students are actively engaged in scientific learning. The unit he chooses to showcase concerns kinetic molecular theory. In the first lesson—a favorite of Underwood and his students—students act out molecules to simulate the notion that (according to kinetic molecular theory) molecules in a closed system are always moving.

To start the lesson, Underwood has students "become molecules," moving constantly at a constant speed to indicate that they all exist at the same temperature. He has students move around the room until they run into obstructions, at which point they "bounce off." Underwood helps students understand that the "bouncing" represents force exerted on a container—"That's the pressure. P." The amount of space students take up is volume (V). The number of students is the number of molecules (N). R is a constant, and the average speed at which students travel is temperature (T). With this as a foundation, Underwood helps students understand the equation PV=NRT.

Continuing the lesson, Underwood gives students directions to have them act out possible scenarios. When the "temperature goes up," students walk faster; they hit the wall harder; they understand that pressure rises with temperature. By changing the variables (increasing volume, or space; increasing the number of molecules or students) the class learns the concepts of kinetic molecular theory.

Underwood really likes this approach. "It's meaningful to students. They understand it, and it's fun!" When he reflects on the lesson in light of the National Board standards, he is pleased.

However, a videotape of the lesson catches Underwood by surprise. As much as he and the students liked the lesson, the tape reveals that they were having fun more than they were learning. He explains:

> *I was really thinking that would be the best lesson to include in my portfolio, because it fits in perfectly with the National Board standards. It's got authentic learning . . . it's kinesthetic. . . . But then you really look at it and you see it's just a bunch of kids walking around bumping into each other. And they're more interested in bumping into each other than they are in whether PV=NRT.*

Most importantly, Underwood discovers the students aren't grasping the concept. Watching the video, he says aloud, "You can tell they're not getting it."

Unable to call this his "best lesson" any longer, Underwood goes back to the drawing board. He creates a new series of lessons—this time incorporating high-impact demonstrations. Underwood has students draw their understanding of the concepts to showcase their learning. He sees a big change in the new videotape.

> *You can see the thinking processes that they're going through as they're drawing. They ask good questions and they're fascinated by the concept. It's the same exact concept as in the acting activity, but . . . they internalize it a lot better.*

As a result of his new lesson, Underwood has shifted the tone from fun to fascination about science and kinetic molecular theory.

Debriefing the case. This case shows the National Board process at its best: helping teachers see the strengths and weaknesses of their teaching, motivating them to make changes as needed, and emphasizing the critical importance of student learning. Underwood took the process seriously. As a result, his lessons improved and his students got more out of his class. Unfortunately, there is more to the picture when other teachers' experiences in similar situations are considered; some of their comments are discussed below to illustrate the full reality of reflecting with the aid of videotape as part of the National Board process.

Did reflection take place? By all accounts, Underwood did reflect on his practice. At first, he felt good about his lesson on kinetic molecular theory. But seeing his practice on the videotape, he discovered a critical problem that he had previously missed. He learned that there was more work to do before the lesson, the learning, and the entry were complete. Having revamped his unit, he was more confident in explaining what he was doing with his students, why, and how it impacted their learning.

What supported or hindered reflection? This case is particularly instructive for revealing the benefits of structured reflection. Three aspects of the process especially supported Underwood's reflection in this case. First, he used the National Board standards to assess the lesson and realized that in many ways it was pedagogically strong. Second, he used the videotape to get a new perspective on the lesson—a perspective that changed his opinion. Third, he focused heavily on a question of paramount significance to the National Board: "How does the lesson advance student learning?" This combination of elements supported a reflective process Underwood didn't achieve on his own. Significantly, the results not only impacted his students that year, but the following year, when he chose to use the new and improved unit again.

How did the reflection contribute to teaching? Examining videotapes of the lessons changed Underwood's perception of the unit, the lessons themselves, and their impacts on students, suggesting that he found the activity not only reflective, but also highly valuable. That he kept the changes in his unit the next year reinforces the long-lasting effect reflection can have on teaching. Underwood described the results himself: "[The students] seem to be enjoying the class more and they're definitely learning [the concept] better. . . . They're getting it a lot quicker and, I think, in a lot more depth." If not for the chance to see the lesson in a new way, Underwood would have thought the lesson was successful and would have seen no reason to reflect on it further. "I've always liked that whole section," he said, adding, "If I hadn't really been thoughtful about it, I wouldn't have" changed anything. If Underwood's experience is any indication, the benefits of this kind of reflection hold real promise for teaching.

However, the other teachers' experiences cast a shadow over this case's success. They found that videotaping sometimes added little more to their lessons than the evidence required to show the National Board they had met standards. Whether or not the teachers benefited from examining lessons on videotape, the tapes themselves were still required as evidence

for the National Board—a nonreflective component of a supposedly reflective activity. Green's experience sent her on a veritable rampage.

> I don't own a video camera. Or any equipment. So I have the video pro-
> ductions class here at the high school come down. Do you think I can get a
> good tape? [She laughs.] Oh, my God! So then I'm starting screaming and
> pulling my hair out. I can't believe how hard it is to get this stupid video!
> You get to just the perfect place in your curriculum where you have a les-
> son that shows all these things, because they don't just happen every day.
> So I'm like, wow, I'm right here at this unit, and this shows this problem-
> solving piece, it shows the application, it shows this, this, this. I'd have the
> person come in to tape, and then you've got to get your room sort of
> arranged. Oh, the battery ran out in the middle of the tape. Oh, the next time
> they come, they forgot to turn the mike on. Oh, they set the auto zoom, so
> every time they zoomed in to look at somebody, the whole screen went
> dark. Oh, I mean, every single tape they took screwed up. I couldn't believe
> it! I'm like, oh, my God! I'm never going to get this done!

In this worst-case scenario, the practicalities of videotaping eclipsed its
value as a reflective tool. Unlike Underwood's satisfying experience, this
example doesn't mention any new learning on Green's part—only sheer
exasperation. Green acknowledged that creating the lessons for videotape
benefited her teaching and her students, but one has to wonder if the same
benefit cannot be achieved without overemphasis on technical issues.

What can we learn from this case? Taking both Underwood's and the
other teachers' experiences into account, we see that encouraging reflection by having teachers videotape and analyze practice has a positive
side and a negative side. At times, examining lessons on videotape
proved to be a potent element of the portfolio. The teachers believed the
process to have the potential to affect teaching in lasting and powerful
ways, by prompting reflection and encouraging subsequent change. But
its benefits had attendant drawbacks that also detracted from its perceived value. The skills, equipment, time, and infinite patience needed to
record practice while teaching, even though it fostered reflection,
seemed excessive to some of the teachers. Those wishing to support
teachers' reflection may wish to adopt videotape as a valuable medium,
but must also balance it with the support needed to make the experience
manageable, too.

For Underwood, analyzing his teaching with the aid of the videotape was a highly reflective activity—even if the videotaping process caused angst in general among the teachers. In the next case, we see a similar pattern when King constructed an entry requiring her to analyze student work. Again we see that the reflective process had merit, but that practical aspects of entry creation can present a burden without improving practice.

Case #2: Analyzing Student Work

One entry in King's portfolio calls for students to make "real world connections" in their social studies learning. To showcase this aspect of her teaching, King chooses an assignment in which students create visual representations of abstract concepts, such as "rights" and "power." After the lesson, she collects samples of the students' responses to the assignment, spreading cartoons and drawings all over the room. She then sets about figuring out what samples of student learning she needs—"two pieces of this and two pieces of that"—to satisfy the National Board. She sorts through the stacks until at last she has selected just the right samples to analyze.

Now she is ready to work. King looks at the student samples closely for evidence of their understanding. This student "can't express this concept verbally, but she can certainly express it in a drawing," she notices, looking at one. The next student's understanding is reversed. Of a third student, she points out, "He totally missed some aspect that's not there at all. It's not in the written work; it's not in the visual work. It's just not there." King sees that for students like this, she needs to reteach the concept. As she continues analyzing the students' work, she writes careful notes on each student's assignment, for these will be included as evidence of her teaching in the entry.

Debriefing the case. By the end of this case, we can see glimmers of the impact this reflection had on King's teaching. Analyzing the student work helped King see whether students were grasping abstract concepts. Given the importance of teachers' awareness of student progress, this seems like a worthwhile endeavor. But King's impressions of this element of the portfolio largely limited its advantages to the one-time certification process.

Did reflection take place? King described this process as reflective; she used the information to inform and direct her practice. Looking at the work samples helped her see her practice in a new light—one that simply teaching the lesson couldn't offer.

But it should be noted that only *part* of the process was reflective. In King's opinion, the early steps of the activity were essentially nonreflective. "That was not a reflective process so much as it was sorting. . . . Once I had [the work] sorted, then I started to say, okay, these won't do, these will do. . . . So it's materials choice as opposed to reflection."

Only after this phase of the activity was completed did King analyze the pieces of work—the activity that did involve reflection.

What supported or hindered reflection? Only the videotape of his practice helped Underwood get a new perspective on his teaching, while the student work samples helped King gain a new perspective on hers. Instead of judging the lesson from the standpoint of a teacher, she judged it by the outcomes for the students. Again, the National Board had structured an activity—using standards and specific questions to guide teachers' thinking—that both motivated and supported their reflection.

How did the reflection contribute to teaching? The fact that King used the information gleaned from analysis of student work to reteach concepts to students who had missed them suggested that this was not only a reflective but also a fairly valuable experience—not just for her, but for her students. Her own words confirmed this interpretation. She called her reflection on the students' work "revealing" and added, "I thought about it a lot more that year than I do most years."

Despite apparent advantages to analyzing student work, the teachers as a group had mixed feelings about the process. On one hand, the exercise made them learn about students and think about how to help them. For instance, Nichols agreed with King, saying that this kind of analysis was "much deeper than what we do most of the time." Green noted that analyzing student work in the manner required by the National Board made her "clearly sit down and focus on it," and Underwood called the process "very valuable." The teachers' words suggested that they all found the activity meaningful.

However, as with the other activities of the National Board portfolio, that the activity was reflective and valuable didn't mean it was easy to pull off, especially because of technical requirements. One particularly challenging issue was time. Nichols found the process of responding to students' work so carefully "extremely time consuming." Underwood estimated it took him six hours to look at the two students' work over the course of a month; King noted that to do such careful analysis for her hundred and fifty students would be impossible. Despite its advantages, she admitted, "There's no way to do any kind of realistic reflection that would involve even most of them."

Generally, the teachers felt that analyzing student work was a reflective and beneficial activity that was unlikely to occur in the usual life of a teacher. Said King, "If you could do that for more kids, you [would] get a better sense of where they're coming from and what their strengths and weaknesses are and all the things that you're supposed to be doing." Her opinion is a disappointing conclusion about analyzing student work, given the teachers' beliefs about the process's potential benefits for students. The large numbers of students for which secondary teachers are responsible simply don't allow time for in-depth analysis of student work on a regular basis.

What can we learn from this case? As in the previous case, reflection involving analyzing student work had its pros and cons. The teachers certainly appreciated the learning they gained in thoroughly analyzing student work, but the actual results of the reflection for students—at least for these experienced teachers—were relatively minor. Moreover, the teachers saw the process of such close analysis as unrealistic—a lengthy process they were willing to endure for the sake of certification, but would hardly be able to manage in the day-to-day time constraints of teaching.

Nevertheless, this case reveals that to conduct such analysis *at all*—even one year for the sake of a portfolio—can have a significant impact on both teachers and students. Small changes in lessons over time can have a huge impact on student learning, as we saw in Underwood's example in the previous case. For a teacher to achieve meaningful analysis of student work can raise awareness of student learning in a way that can potentially enhance instruction and learning in years to come.

Unlike the deep changes in practice in Underwood's case and the greater awareness of student understanding in King's, such meaningful outcomes are not always so prevalent. The next case shows vividly what happens when teachers already meet National Board standards but have a hard time constructing convincing evidence to prove they do.

Case #3: Reflecting on Standards

Green's portfolio calls for her to show the National Board that her teaching helps students to think and reason deeply in mathematics. Immediately, Green thinks of the perfect lesson. She chooses one in which students "inherit" $20,000 and a piece of property outside town. They then use trigonometry to design a farm with their imaginary windfall. Green supplies information from local stores on which students perform calculations, figuring out "how many fence posts they'll need, how many linear feet of fencing, how much seed," and so on. The goal is to calculate the cost and decide whether the farm will be profitable. In Green's mind the lesson meets the National Board standards and will easily satisfy the requirements of the entry.

As it turns out, Green can't submit the lesson, simply because she has trouble videotaping the evidence. Frustrated, she cries, "The videotape didn't work! . . . I decided to forget it. That's not going to go."

Green starts over. She chooses another lesson—a statistics activity using bags of M&Ms to practice probability. Again, she reflects on the lesson in light of the standards. Again she feels assured of the lesson's excellence, but again has to reject it as an entry. This time, although it is "a wonderful activity," Green doesn't feel she can evidence "deep reasoning"—important since "reasoning and thinking mathematically" is the National Board standard required for the entry. Green knows the students have in fact met this standard, but she hasn't collected adequate proof to send to the National Board.

Trying a third time, Green chooses yet another lesson. Again, she considers her practice in light of the standards, this time choosing a calculus lesson—an application of infinite limits—for the entry. She incorporates literature by reading a relevant, comical skit ("Zero's Paradox") from Gödel, Escher, and Bach (e.g., Hofstadter, 1979) that illustrates the concept. She has students work with paper to reinforce their learning, guiding them in "cutting it in half, and cutting it in half . . . and looking at what happens. Can you keep cutting it in half? Is there a pattern? Are you going to reach a limit?" Next, she has the students work with the concepts by using cardboard boxes, so that they can visually see the concept of minimum and maximum limits. Finally, she has students work with infinite limits using formulas, graphs, and curves to reinforce the mathemat-

ics. Green summarizes the set of activities: "I brought in the idea of limits with philosophy, with shapes, and with graphical and algebraic representation." Finally, all of the pieces—the mathematical concepts, the National Board standards, and the evidence—come together in one satisfactory entry.

Debriefing the case. In this case, the modifications Green made for a portfolio exceeded the goals of the lesson. A significant amount of extra time and effort was required to show the National Board she met the standard—time not spent to benefit the students. Her thoughts about the outcome are complex, as seen in the discussion below.

Did reflection take place? Determining whether a lesson met the standard necessarily required reflection. Green described her mental process:

> I read through the National Board standards [and asked,] "Do I do these things in the classroom?" [One standard was] knowledge of mathematics. Yes, I think I'm very knowledgeable in mathematics. . . . Knowledge of teaching Practice, I know how to teach in a classroom. . . . Reasoning and thinking mathematically . . . when I read through that, I'm like, sure, I do those things.

Green saw these standards reflected in her practice in general, which helped her to become clearer on what she was doing and why. She also believed that each of three lessons she wanted to use for her entry met these National Board standards. And yet her entry still wasn't done. The nonreflective components of the entry required more work.

What supported or hindered reflection? No obstacles hindered Green's reflection, as time constraints and external demands did so often in other cases described throughout this book. The standards supported her reflection and helped her see her lessons more objectively—just as they did for Underwood and King in the previous two cases. What this case adds, however, is the recognition that reflection on standards may not be as meaningful when teachers already meet those standards. In this case, Green believed her reflection helped her teaching grow from *meeting* standards to *exceeding* standards—certainly a benefit for student learning, but one that came at the expense of inordinate planning. In other cases, the teachers found that the standards simply confirmed what they were already doing well. Having to prove their accomplishment, however, was another story altogether. We see again in this case how extensive nonreflective aspects of portfolio creation can be.

How was the reflection valuable to teaching? Speaking of this experience, Green had mixed feelings about its value. On one hand, she could see that the reflective process served to validate her teaching—a meaningful affirmation of practice. On the other, the modifications and technical adjustments needed to create a satisfactory entry became both redundant and time consuming, without significantly improving student learning.

"Significantly" here is a key word, for Green acknowledged some improvement in her lessons after she refined them for the National Board. Specifically, she believed that having students describe their thinking processes in writing to evidence their mathematical reasoning benefited their learning.

> It truly helps the students get at a deeper meaning by forcing them to [write out their reasoning]. I knew every student had to have this particular understanding, and I could see on paper whether a student understood it or not. Those things are not trivial. They actually help your classroom and they help your students learn.

Nevertheless, to have such reasoning written down was a requirement of the National Board, not a goal of Green's teaching. She later argued that students' reasoning might be even stronger if they *didn't* write their reasoning. To illustrate, she gave an example from her practice of a strategy she used long before learning of the National Board.

> In calculus classes, I give oral exams. . . . They have to be able to explain the concepts in calculus and how they interrelate. That's something I would never have evidence of, and it's not something I have students write down, because it's important that they be able to verbalize and explain. They'll do that in much more detail if they talk about it than if they have to write it on paper. . . . I get more reasoning by having them verbalize.

Once her portfolio was complete, Green felt relieved that she didn't "have to worry about the evidence" and could once again assess students' reasoning orally. Green believed her usual, oral approach to discovering students' reasoning was as effective as, if not more effective than, the approach she had to use for the National Board. As she put it, "There is a balance between when to have them solve problems, when to have them write, and when to have them speak." Without the pressure of the assessment requirements, she was free again to make the professional choice about when to take which approach.

What can we learn from this case? Green's thoughts on this entry illustrate the complicated feelings that all of the teachers expressed about adapting their lessons for the sake of the National Board. To summarize, Green believed she was already meeting National Board standards with all of her lessons in terms of student reasoning, which she could tell by their verbal responses. But because she had to include concrete evidence of their reasoning, she changed her lessons (strictly for that purpose) to have students write their reasoning down. Even though she adapted her lesson only to satisfy formatting requirements, she believed the effort made a difference in students' understanding. However, as in the lesson with limits discussed above, she still saw the student writing as an "extra" piece of the lesson that wouldn't normally be part of her teaching.

Green's experience of repeatedly adjusting lessons was echoed by the other teachers, who experienced similar sequences of events at one time or another while creating their portfolios: Underwood when he had to change the way he ran classroom discussions (even though he liked his own way better than the National Board's) and King and Nichols when they had to rearrange their classrooms to make better videotapes (even though the new arrangements didn't necessarily improve the lessons). Overall, the example illustrated a general belief on the part of the teachers that they did reflect on their practice in light of the standards and that that process in and of itself was worth doing. But perhaps the reason the teachers didn't all extol the benefits of the changes was related to a comment Green made that, while the changes were admittedly positive, "That cost-benefit ratio is just not there." In other words, the effort required to make such changes didn't always justify the results for student learning. In everyday teaching, time is of the essence. And yet, when teachers take the time, it seems that to refine lessons with such attention and such high standards of teaching can also bring teaching and learning to an entirely new level.

SUMMARY

Describing their process of achieving National Board certification, the four teachers all found it reflective. The teachers all believed they learned something from the process, although some claimed to have learned more than others. Overall, the experience of rigorous, standards-based reflection through the use of written commentary, videotaped lessons, and student work was a generally valuable journey of growth and discovery, even though the conditions were grueling, time consuming, and expensive. The National Board certification process is designed specifically for highly accomplished teachers, making it appropriate for teachers in advanced stages of their careers. Additionally, the uncompromising particulars of a high-stakes assessment, associated with issues of validity, reliability, and fairness, make it impractical for everyday use in programs of teacher learning. However, some of the core activities involved in the portfolio process, such as comparing practice with standards and analyzing student work, seem manageable for teachers to take on as habits of reflective practice. These same activities appeared in the teachers' descriptions of other programs in which they were involved. Such programs are the focus of the next chapter, which discusses a less formal, yet structured approach: a voluntary program for teacher assessment.

Chapter Thirteen

A Voluntary Program for Teacher Assessment

Are teachers committed to reflection when the stakes are low? In the previous chapter, we saw reflection in the context of National Board certification—a rigorous, high-stakes assessment. What happens when teachers participate in similar activities without the pressure and accountability? This chapter's case addresses this question.

New forms of teacher assessment incorporate activities designed to foster reflection. Like the National Board certification process, these systems combine assessment and professional growth by having teachers study their own practice by gathering evidence and comparing practice with standards. King voluntarily participated in a district-level pilot for such a program, in which teachers became familiar with the program without the pressure to succeed that accompanied the National Board process.

A CASE OF A VOLUNTARY PROGRAM FOR TEACHER ASSESSMENT

The single case included in this chapter offers a contrasting example to the teachers' experiences with the National Board. Unlike the nationally organized, highly structured National Board process, the district-based program King experienced relied more heavily on teachers to get the program off the ground. In the next case, we see how King and her colleagues fared as they took on this responsibility.

Case #1: Enhancing Professional Practice

After school on the first Tuesday of the month, an all-call comes over the P.A. system: "Will all teachers involved in the pilot teacher evaluation please meet in Mr. Standall's room? All teachers involved in the pilot teacher evaluation, please meet in Mr. Standall's room." There, in Mr. Standall's room, three teachers in the pilot group sit chatting to see if anyone else will arrive. No one does.

After covering a few unrelated issues—like the controversial student-designed logo for the prom—the teachers get out their materials for the pilot program. King immediately raises two administrative matters. Has a computer problem been solved, so that teachers can use the Internet aspect of the program? Has the district coordinator ordered extra books for new teachers joining the group? The teachers divide up tasks to call the district and get these issues resolved so they can proceed.

Moving to more substantive matters, one of the teachers pulls out a binder that contains evidence for two of her goals. She tells her colleagues, "This doesn't feel like an evaluation, but like you're learning from the process." She believes the program is helping her see when something in her practice isn't working. "And if something isn't working, then I'll change it. So I think it's good." The others nod in agreement. Then the conversation moves toward external resistance to the model. One teacher, a union representative, says that those "whining" about the program don't understand it—nor do they show up to these meetings. Having lasted forty-five minutes, the meeting ends.

The following month, the threesome reconvenes. A new teacher joins them. King describes the process of gathering evidence, talking over what they've done, and giving each other suggestions. She calls the process "reflective" and asserts that teachers committed to the program will be "learning a lot—it could be a growth spurt."

The new teacher likes the concept of the model and compares it with some of the other evaluations she has experienced, which she found more subjective and less professional. The teachers share horror stories of poorly executed evaluations they've experienced over the years. After forty-five minutes, the teachers drift out and the meeting sputters to a close.

Debriefing the case. This case demonstrates what can happen when teachers are given a program encouraging reflection and invited to participate voluntarily. On one hand, the case provides evidence that the teachers have been reflecting on their own, outside the meeting. Their hearty endorsement of the process as being valuable to teachers' growth supports the effectiveness of this process. On the other hand, the case shows how the lack of a formal meeting structure can lead to a vague sense of purpose. Little if any reflection takes place in the context of the meeting; rather, teachers briefly share their efforts and then get distracted by other topics.

Did reflection take place? As noted earlier, this case contrasts with the teachers' National Board experiences, especially in the reflection that took place.

King described the pilot program explicitly, saying that the "model [does] involve reflection. . . . It does require small groups of teachers to get together and talk about teaching." An examination of the program's materials revealed an emphasis on reflection as a standard of professional practice, and one that is enhanced by teacher collaboration. Activities supported this emphasis, encouraging reflection in a number of ways: setting goals, providing evidence of meeting them, and discussing them in small groups.

Interestingly, despite the teachers' favorable opinions of the program and explicit claims that it could be reflective, evidence revealed the potential had not yet been realized. The teachers' individual efforts may have been reflective, but their collaborative venture was not. As was true with the activities affiliated with the National Board, the reflective opportunities posed by the program were associated with nonreflective counterparts that took time and effort without necessarily impacting teaching or learning.

What supported or hindered reflection? The reflection that did take place in this case was supported in several ways. The model provided a great deal of technical support. In meetings in which King discussed the program with other teachers, it was evident that the book *Enhancing Professional Practice* (Danielson, 1996) explained the framework, described four domains of teaching in detail, and outlined a collaborative structure for self-assessment. Software to support the program was also available to guide teachers' reflection. The teachers were therefore supported by standards, materials, and guidelines. The teachers also had the opportunity to talk about their practice with other teachers using the framework. In these ways, reflection was supported.

But reflection was also hindered in this case in significant ways. In two sequential meetings, the teachers spent almost all of their time organizing the pilot effort, instead of participating in the collaborative activities that were part of the program. Related tasks included searching for teachers to participate, setting meeting dates, getting materials from the district, getting software to work, and responding to criticism of the program. Time was also a factor. By the time teachers settled into the meeting and took care of administrative tasks, the meeting time had usually run out. Reflective activities affiliated with the program were easily pushed aside in favor of the business side of the pilot.

An additional matter, and one that was harder to address, is that the teachers in the pilot group seemed uncertain of how to engage in substantial reflection. Any collaborative conversation they did hold consisted primarily of reporting out and holding up their binders. They had selected their personal goals and shared their chosen domains, but neglected to create a culture of collaboration to support their reflection—another feature of the program. In the absence of this element, just "checking in" with each other became the routine.

How was reflection valuable to teaching? King described the program as a potential learning experience. All of the teachers identified advantages of the process that made it worthwhile. One particularly appreciated being able to choose the area on which she wanted to concentrate. For her, this model helped her learn in and from practice, which resulted in positive change. Another teacher quoted the program materials as saying that a teacher who could meet the program standard would be a good teacher, suggesting that ongoing reflection on standards of practice would contribute to quality teaching.

What can we learn from this case? A few key points can be made about the nonreflective activities in this case. First, without the practical support of the district and administration, the teachers became responsible for attending to practical matters like how to get materials. This feature was a commonality with the National Board process, which also required teachers to spend a great deal of time on technical matters that did little to advance teacher learning and reflection. These activities took up time that could have been spent on the reflective activities the teachers said were so valuable.

Second, without some kind of facilitation or leadership to guide the conversation, the teachers seemed to drift easily off topic, away from reflecting on practice and toward complaints and anecdotes about how things had been in the past. The pilot program contained many of the activities that sparked reflection and learning in teachers during the National Board process, such as comparing practice to standards and analyzing student work. Yet, it expected teachers to engage in these activities without the support of materials, guidelines, or directions to help teachers stay focused. As witnessed in the pilot evaluation meetings, this loss of focus sometimes resulted in limited learning.

Third, without some reason for doing otherwise, the teachers seemed to lack the motivation for setting and achieving their goals. Unlike the National Board process, in which teachers explicitly stated that they were reflecting in order to complete an entry of a high-stakes assessment that they were motivated to complete, this pilot evaluation was a low-stakes endeavor. It was so low-stakes, in fact, that administrators and other teachers barely seemed to notice its existence. In such an environment, it seemed entirely possible that, when it came to the activities of the pilot, the teachers could either take them or leave them with absolutely no cost to themselves.

Overall, without these kinds of supports or conditions in place, even the potentially reflective, thoroughly designed aspects of the Danielson model made it difficult to actualize. The fate of the program would remain unsettled until voted on by the union. King herself seemed to be reserving judgment on the program. She described herself as being "interested to see" whether the pilot would ever become accepted as a program by the district, especially because, as she said, "the question [on the minds of teachers] will be, 'I see, when do we do this?'" In her mind, even if the pilot were reflective and valuable, and even if it were to pass the union vote, it would still face the obstacles of time with which the teachers seemed constantly to struggle. As was also true with the National Board portfolio process, even potentially valuable experiences were associated with trade-offs that teachers wouldn't necessarily be willing to make.

SUMMARY

The voluntary district program for teacher assessment experienced by King encouraged self-assessment through the use of goals and evidence and was supported by a variety of media for reflection, including conversation, thought, and writing—in theory, if not necessarily in practice.

Along with the opportunity and the intended means of support came a need for assistance. The teachers spearheading the initiative described above were responsible for the areas of recruitment, marketing, administrative details, and politics—leaving little room for the reflection the program was meant to foster. With limited administrative support and a questionable future for the program, its success was far from assured. Nevertheless, the teachers pressed on with efforts to launch an assessment system in their district that they believed could be valuable for teachers. In all, King's experience as described in this case upheld a theme in this chapter that nonreflective components of reflective opportunities could interfere with the opportunities themselves.

Chapter Fourteen

Mentoring Programs

When do teachers learn to reflect? An essential, if somewhat hidden, element of learning to teach, reflection is often fostered in mentoring programs. Although less explicit than the other programs described in this section, such as the programs for teacher assessment, mentors structure the inherently evaluative relationship between master and novice in a way that makes them genuinely valuable in the eyes of teachers.

At least one mentoring relationship stood out as a reflective experience for each of the four teachers while they were learning to teach. In Green's opinion, it was actually the only time that teachers *could* learn to reflect. As she said: "The only way in the public setting that they even try to get [teachers] to be reflective is through the mentoring process."

CASES OF MENTORING PROGRAMS

Three versions of the mentoring process are included in the cases discussed in this chapter: the student-teacher/cooperating-teacher relationship, from a student teacher's point of view; the same relationship from a cooperating teacher's point of view; and a colleague-to-colleague mentoring relationship between two experienced teachers. The cases show the potential for these arrangements to support reflection, even if it isn't always realized.

Case #1: The Student Teacher's Perspective on Learning to Teach

Eleven years ago, Green began her teaching career as a student teacher. She speaks of her cooperating teacher with fondness, calling

119

him the "perfect cooperating teacher. . . . He's just so supportive." Her appreciation of her cooperating teacher stems from a powerful apprenticeship.

Young Green's cooperating teacher habitually walked her through a series of questions that helped her to reflect and to learn the importance of thinking about her practice. She later describes his approach: "He sits in the back, and he watches me and takes notes. Detailed notes. Then he offers, 'Here's what you did well, and here are some things you might try.'" Her description reveals that Green was learning reflective practice when her cooperating teacher used his notes to show her what she was doing in her teaching, in a system that can be viewed as his program for helping her learn.

Debriefing the case. This short case illustrates a familiar student-teaching activity in which the cooperating teacher observes the student teacher teaching, then engages her in reflection in hopes of improving her practice. We see in this scenario the same reflective process Green described herself going through earlier in this book to solve a puzzle of practice on her own. That she learned to reflect in a way that has lasted her entire career validates her cooperating teacher's approach as a valuable model.

Did reflection take place? The answer to this question is an obvious "yes," especially given that Green provided this example to describe how she learned to reflect. In her memory, reflecting on her practice was part of the program of learning to teach—a program designed by her cooperating teacher that has stayed with Green her entire career. Elaborating, Green explained that reflecting in this way had helped her think deeply about her practice. Even in mundane tasks like grading, Green used an inquisitive, philosophical approach in which she asked meaningful questions ("What does this final grade mean? Or, What should it mean?") instead of taking the easiest approach. She believed in addressing such issues thoughtfully, but worried that, with other teachers, "they're never, ever discussed." Green's cooperating teacher helped make reflection a part of her everyday life. He helped her learn how to think and ask questions as she learned how to teach.

What supported or hindered reflection? Green's cooperating teacher provided a model for supporting reflection—a system of observation, debriefing, questioning, and moving forward to new ideas for improving teaching. Other important if subtle elements included a safe and nurturing relationship and a willingness on Green's part to learn.

What happens when these conditions aren't present? Green gave an unfortunate example. She witnessed a student teacher in her school performing poorly throughout his internship. Despite his cooperating teacher's efforts to reflect with him on his practice, Green said, this student teacher "would do his own thing." Green linked the apparently poor quality of the student teacher's practice directly to his refusal to reflect on his practice, even though he was prompted to do so by the cooperating teacher. Her anecdote made the point that, even though cooperating teachers may prepare an informal program of reflection for student teachers, the interns won't necessarily cooperate.

The end of the story is similarly discouraging. The cooperating teacher wouldn't recommend the student teacher for a position, yet he was certified and hired in another district. Halfway through the year, he was fired. Green's frustration with this reality was evident: "Come on! So where's the reflection?" In her view, reflection was called for not just in a student teacher's practice, but in hiring quality teachers, as well.

How did the reflection contribute to teaching? That Green found her student teaching experience meaningful is clear in her recollection of the learning that took place at the time. Green never forgot the process her cooperating teacher taught; she made it a part of her own teaching and even used it as a mentor for new teachers.

> I watch them teach and I take notes; I tell them what they did well and I tell them how I would have taught the lesson and why. [I ask], Why did you do it this way? What do you think the students learned from that? And I say, I teach it this way, because of these reasons.

In these words, Green tied her own approach to coaching new teachers to her cooperating teacher's, suggesting that she found the process valuable from both perspectives—as a student and as a cooperating teacher. In fact, she said she believed this model of questioning was one of few ways to help teachers reflect. "Doing what you do for your reason, and then hearing someone else's reason for doing it . . . that's almost the only way to grow."

What can we learn from this case? From Green's experience, we see that student teaching can support reflective practice. By nature, the process is evaluative, providing implicit motivations to compel student teachers to carefully consider what they are doing and why. While a cooperating teacher's efforts may not guarantee that reflection—or quality teaching—will take place, the process of observation and reflective collaboration is a widely accepted part of the program for learning to teach.

Above, we saw the benefits of reflection for student teachers in supportive relationships with their mentors. But what about the cooperating teachers? Does the mentoring relationship hold reflective value for them? This question is addressed in the next case, in which Nichols describes her experience coaching a new student teacher.

Case #2: The Cooperating Teacher's Perspective on Learning to Teach

Student teacher Stephanie Gold is teaching an English lesson for seniors for the first time today. Her cooperating teacher, Mrs. Nichols, sits discreetly at her desk, listening intently and scribbling notes. At the end of the day, the two sit down to debrief the lesson. Nichols begins with effusive praise, pointing out many things Gold has done well—relating to students, adjusting the lesson midstream in response to their questions, and planning a content-rich lesson. She elicits Gold's opinion of the lesson, then shares her perspective as an experienced teacher. By the time the conversation is over, Gold has moved from being nervous and excited about the lesson she has taught to being thoughtful and reflective about what she has done well, what she can do better, and how to apply her learning to her lesson the next day.

Debriefing the case. Nichols's case bears many similarities to the process Green experienced with her cooperating teacher. This time, however, we gain more insight into the effect on the cooperating teacher as she mentors her student teacher, Gold.

Did reflection take place? Judging from the effect of the conversation on the student teacher's thinking, reflection was apparent for Gold. But was it reflective for Nichols? Nichols's explanation reveals her own reflective process in deciding what to do and why as she helped Gold learn to teach. She described her model for debriefing a lesson, including talking and reflecting on what had happened. She explained, "I want to make sure that she knows that she's doing a really good job, and at the same time I want to be able to tell her some things that I think will make her a better teacher. And that helps me be a better teacher, too!" Nichols's suggestions to her student teacher served as good reminders to herself. She exclaimed, "I certainly have room to grow!" In her mind, teaching others to reflect helped her to improve her own teaching, as well.

What supported or hindered reflection? In this and the previous case, key elements supporting reflection are consistent. A system of observation and reflective collaboration, a trusting relationship, and a willingness to improve as teachers supported reflection by both Gold and Nichols.

How was the reflection valuable to teaching? Nichols consistently mentors student teachers, believing it improves her own teaching. "Mentoring a young teacher . . . [is] good for me, because it forces me to be a better teacher." She explained that when student teachers observed her, she needed to be "more 'on'"—better able to defend her practice and more clear about what she was doing and why.

What can we learn from this case? Of importance in this case is Nichols's strong feeling about the benefits of mentoring teachers *for herself*—a veteran of thirty-one years. Having attended years of in-service workshops, aced National Board certification, and even taught university teacher-education courses, this teacher would seem difficult to challenge. And yet, through her own reflection and the process of helping a student teacher to learn to reflect, Nichols was able to challenge herself and constantly improve in her practice. Her case makes the argument that many teachers may benefit from becoming cooperating teachers, if their process is as reflective and self-examining as Nichols's.

Whereas the student-teacher/cooperating-teacher relationship is widely accepted and commonly used in teaching teachers, the peer-helper relationship seen in the next case is more problematic. This approach, which calls for experienced teachers to coach each other, draws heavily on familiar student-teaching models, so successful in the previous two cases. But one teacher's experience reveals that reflection in this context may be more difficult to achieve.

Case #3: The Peer-Helper Relationship

A "new" teacher, Georgia Elliot, has arrived at Eastern High School with twenty years' experience under her belt. Despite her experience, the

*teacher reportedly struggles to be effective. Nichols agrees to work with
the teacher as a peer-helper at the prompting of her principal. To mentor
her colleague, Nichols uses the same technique she uses with student
teachers: observing a class, taking notes, and sharing ideas.*

*Unfortunately, Elliot reacts defensively. She complains to her principal
that Nichols is telling her what to do. She responds harshly to Nichols, lash-
ing out at her for imposing her way of doing things on Elliot. Nichols,
shocked, retreats to examine her role and figure out how to better approach
the situation.*

*Elliot's defensiveness extends beyond the classroom, as Nichols soon
discovers. She appears not to listen in department meetings, instead blurt-
ing out opinions and interjecting her own complaints and assertions.
Nichols considers her mentorship role: Should I say something? Can I
help her with this? Though her concern stems from a loyalty to her mentorship role and a desire to make department meetings effective, Nichols
rejects the idea. "She's been teaching twenty years," she says to herself.
"I'm not going to change her behavior." She decides to let the issue go.
Instead, she cautiously continues her in-classroom observations and
hopes for the relationship to improve.*

Debriefing the case. This case is included as a contrast to the student-
teacher/cooperating-teacher relationship. Whereas such relationships are
usually unquestioned, the peer-helper role Nichols took with a colleague
met with more resistance than she had ever experienced—with conse-
quences for reflection and for the effectiveness of the endeavor.

Did reflection take place? Compared with the reflection in the previous
case, Nichols only hints at reflection with Elliot. The process that takes place
in the classroom—again, observation and collaborative conversation—is
certainly reflective in design. But the process is veiled in a layer of self-
consciousness, as Nichols constantly second-guesses herself in response to
Elliot's reaction. She seems restrained in her enthusiasm to share ideas with
the teacher, fearing the defensive attack. She refrains entirely from approaching matters of school culture (namely, how to contribute effectively in
a department meeting) that would be acceptable training ground for a student
teacher. Instead, Nichols finds herself reflecting privately on the situation
before ever approaching her colleague with a suggestion or a concern—
particularly given her experience, which warned her that approaching this
colleague as a mentor could be a mistake.

What supported or hindered reflection? The arrangement of colleague-to-colleague mentoring provides a structure in which reflection is supposed to be welcome. Yet, Nichols took on her role with more caution than she did as a cooperating teacher, because her partner was an experienced colleague. As a result, reflection was somewhat hindered. Of course, the caution could be due to a personality conflict, instead of a difference between mentoring a preservice teacher and mentoring an experienced teacher. Either way, Nichols seemed to mistrust the relationship. That mistrust constrained her ability to use reflection as a tool for helping a fellow teacher to improve her practice.

How was reflection valuable to teaching? In this situation, nothing Nichols said or did indicated it held value for her teaching. When Nichols held back her comments to Elliot, she sacrificed her ability to help her partner improve her teaching, too. Perhaps in the long run the mentoring relationship held some value, as it had the potential to do. But when compared with her enthusiasm for supporting student teachers in her classroom, Nichols's indifference toward Elliot spoke volumes about her belief in the significance of the relationship.

What can we learn from this case? The peer-helper arrangement in which Nichols participated involved a reflective relationship. However, Nichols didn't seem to find this activity of communicating about practice particularly valuable. Perhaps more importantly, she didn't seem nearly as confident in her ability to guide the reflective activities in this context. Whereas a structure existed for guiding conversations between student teachers and cooperating teachers, no such structure emerged for talking openly with colleagues about sensitive issues. For such relationships to work, they may require the same ingredients important for student teachers and their mentors: an agreed-upon system for reflecting, trust, and a willingness to change.

SUMMARY

In the first two cases described above—Green's as a student teacher and Nichols's as a cooperating teacher—mentoring programs promoted reflection that helped the teachers form independent habits of practice. But in the third—with Nichols as a mentor for an experienced colleague—the program seemed somewhat inhibited. The reflective questions Nichols wanted to ask seemed less welcome, if not consciously avoided. Perhaps that avoidance was due to the nature of the relationship, in which an acclaimed teacher was assigned to her peer. Perhaps it was due to the issue at hand, which in this case was a personal matter. Or perhaps it reflected the common culture of schools, where thoughtful critique is reserved for student teachers and fellow teachers mind their own business. For schools to benefit from a reflective stance to teaching, structures must be put into place that raise expectations, foster trust, and value continuous improvement. Having covered several cases of reflection in the context of different programs of teacher assessment—the National Board process, a voluntary district program for teacher assessment, and mentoring—the discussion now turns to what these programs show us about supporting reflection.

Chapter Fifteen

Reflection and the Conditions of Programs

A REVIEW OF THIS SECTION: REFLECTION AND THE CONDITIONS OF PROGRAMS

In the cases in this section on the programmatic context, we saw a number of activities that successfully motivated reflection. These contrasted with many of the unsuccessful school-based activities in the previous section (the professional context) that sometimes tried and usually failed to engage the teachers. The cases in this section, when they succeeded, did so by engaging the *mind*—supporting teachers in actively and consciously reflecting on their teaching in a way that actually helped them learn.

The cases in this section illustrated a range of reflection in three programs of assessment—the National Board certification process, a voluntary program for teacher assessment, and mentoring programs—each designed to provide opportunities for reflection. Common themes cut across all of the programs that offer some insight as to how and whether reflection occurred in the context of teacher assessment.

The first part of this chapter discusses differences in the place of reflection in these programs as compared with the place of reflection in schools. It also discusses the challenges and benefits of reflection in this context. The next part of this chapter discusses lessons learned from the cases and the advantages and disadvantages to relying on programs of teacher assessment and evaluation to encourage reflective practice.

The Place of Reflection in Programs

In each of the three programs included in this section, reflective practice was granted a special place in the design. Each of the programs explicitly or implicitly encouraged reflection, providing multiple opportunities for teachers to reflect for the sake of the program and, in many cases, a number of structured supports to help them do so.

Each of these programs was in some sense voluntary, meaning that the activities took place beyond the call of duty. As Nichols said about the National Board process, "Even though it's only six months, you're teaching full time. So you're doing that on top of everything else, [including] being a parent and [fulfilling whatever other responsibilities you have]. So I think that it's very difficult." Although this comment speaks to the National Board process, it could also apply to other programs in this section. When and how reflection takes place is closely connected to where programs fit into teachers' lives.

For Underwood, this meant spending 350 to 400 hours on his National Board portfolio after school and on weekends from January to April, including spring break. The other teachers also named Christmas break and evenings as needed time to work on their portfolios. Participation in pilot assessment programs and serving as mentors also took time after school or at lunch—the only unscheduled breaks in each day. As active teachers, all four subjects worked on these projects on top of coaching, advising students, leading departments, and of course, carrying the usual work load of teaching.

These teachers were highly motivated to reflect on their practice when doing so led to national recognition or helped improve teaching in a way they felt was important. But it should not be overlooked that such motivation may be less prevalent for many busy teachers who may not find time for reflection. Underwood explicitly considered how teachers could be encouraged to reflect on their practice on a regular basis, the way he and the others did in the contexts of various programs: "The only way you could do that is if you gave them enough time to do it." Even so, the time still might not be sufficient: "There's just not enough money out there to give someone a two-hour planning time a day." As it did in other contexts, reflection in programs often fell last on the priority list.

The Challenges and Benefits of Reflecting in Programs

In the programmatic context, the line between challenges and benefits of participating became blurred. We see this trend in the categories discussed below: voluntary participation, recognition, professional opportunities, and financial bonuses. Most of these categories apply primarily if not solely to the National Board certification process and less to the other programs—an issue that will be discussed shortly.

Voluntary Participation

Voluntary participation in any activity can be motivating. When people choose their own activities, they act according to interest and will—an approach likely to heighten motivation and participation. In all of the programs—the National Board for Professional Teaching Standards, the district pilot program for teacher evaluation, and the mentoring programs—voluntary participation seemed to enhance teachers' motivation to take the programs (and relevant reflection) more seriously.

In fact, the teachers explicitly acknowledged that something about the National Board process motivated them to challenge themselves. For Underwood, one reason was, "Ego! I wanted to be the first teacher to [get certified in my area] in the state." For Green, it was professional recognition: "In this profession, all their lives, [teachers] never get any recognition for their work. Ever. And they want it. . . . To me, National Board says, yes, you do all these things [that accomplished teachers do] . . . and I wanted the recognition that I did." Nichols described herself as "always interested in trying something new and different." She also saw the importance of modeling this for students. "I'm a risk taker. And I want my [students] to know that they need to be risk takers, too." Finally, King said that seeking National Board certification was about accepting the challenge; she thought she met the standards and decided to prove it.

These comments revealed that the teachers felt intrinsically motivated to challenge themselves for one reason or another. This seemed critical to the success of the programs, especially compared with cases in which motivation was missing. For example, King's systematic analysis of practice against National Board standards was sincere and meaningful compared with her half-hearted, even falsified response to similar task in her department meeting mentioned earlier in this book. In the context of the programs, the teachers were motivated to take the activity seriously; in the context of their department meetings, they were not. That the teachers voluntarily chose to participate in these programs suggested an internal motivation, making it more likely that they would learn from the experience.

On the negative side, however, voluntary participation can have the effect of limiting participation. This seemed evident only when the teachers compared themselves with other teachers they knew in their schools. For example, Nichols and King (both close to retirement) said they volunteered to take part in the National Board process for the personal challenge. King volunteered to take part in the pilot program out of personal interest. Green and Nichols both volunteered to mentor other teachers because they saw serving as teacher educators as part of their professional roles. But the teachers didn't believe all teachers would feel as intrinsically motivated. Nichols explained:

> [The reason for National Board certification] is to raise the standard of teachers. That's the upside. The downside is it will never be mandatory. It's an issue for the National Board, and they don't want it to be mandatory. There are only going to be certain teachers, and those are only going to be the most driven. But what about all the other [teachers out there]? What are they going to do?

In her opinion, the process was "too threatening" and many teachers didn't "feel secure enough" to take the risk of applying for such a challenging certificate.

Perhaps for this reason, a number of benefits were offered to encourage teachers to take part in the programs—particularly the National Board. The teachers' comments about these benefits—including recognition, professional opportunities, and financial bonuses—provided a sense of the encouragement used to entice teachers to participate.

Recognition

One teacher, Green, believed that many teachers wanted to achieve National Board certification for "the professional recognition, because nobody [else] gives it." She believed this benefit was so important that the lack of recognition was actually "one of the reasons a lot of teachers leave the profession." If her hunch was right, then recognition could be a potentially powerful encouragement for participation.

However, Green herself had not received recognition from her school since becoming National Board certified. Even though she had received national recognition (via the certificate), state recognition (including several luncheons with the governor), and district recognition (in the form of a luncheon and a plaque), she received absolutely no recognition for her certification at her school and she believed administrators there "couldn't care less." Thus, recognition was a benefit for teachers participating in the program only when it was actually given.

Professional Opportunities

Green also spoke on the subject of professional opportunities—a benefit she received from National Board certification that she believed she couldn't have gotten otherwise. For her, this included becoming involved as an instructor in a teacher-education program at a local university, participation in a grant, an invitation to coauthor a book, and facilitation for other National Board candidates.

> I've always been active in my profession. So what it's done for me is allowed me to go out and make contacts and people listen to me now. [The local university] could have used me any time in the last fourteen years. But they never would have thought to, because oh, I'm just some math teacher. But now that I have that credential that tells them [I am] one of the best math teachers you can hook your students up with, then they listen. That's [what's] ironic about it. I've always been good. But nobody cared. Well, they didn't know, and they didn't care.

Later, she added, "[When] I got that [National Board certificate], I could go forward with what I wanted to do." Both King and Underwood similarly said they had their eyes out for opportunities that were open to them once they were certified.

Financial Bonuses

All of the teachers certified when these four teachers were certified received a 15% salary bonus allotted by the legislature for two consecutive years. Although this amount was not insignificant to the teachers, the bonus was reduced to $3,500 per year for two years the year after the teachers were certified, and remained as such until the decision could be reviewed with each legislative session.

King spoke to this issue, saying she was "stinging" in the reduction of the bonus. She believed it would impact whether teachers went through the process, and started adding up the figures.

> If I were a new teacher right now, I could look at it and say, if I put myself through all this and pay the money or coax someone to pay it for me, it's going to cost $2,200. If I [get certified] I'll get $3500 the first year, $3500 the second year; that comes to $7000, and now it's over and done with. Now—I could go finish that MBA or sign on with [another company] or [go into educational consulting].

Her comments implied that the financial bonuses couldn't compete with financial incentives elsewhere that could draw teachers right out of the profession. She acknowledged, "That's not the National Board's problem. That's society's problem." Her comment says much about the effectiveness of relatively small financial incentives. Until the financial bonus was both bigger and secure, King didn't believe it would encourage teachers to participate in the program.

As noted earlier, the examples above were almost entirely drawn from the teachers' discussions about the National Board process. This raises a question as to how the thoughts expressed here apply to the other programs discussed in this section. However, the programs all shared certain elements that make these comments applicable across all of the cases. Perhaps more importantly, the absence of commentary on the part of the teachers regarding the other voluntary programs and mentoring programs also sent a message that the strengths, benefits, and challenges associated with those programs were less significant, if they were offered at all.

LESSONS LEARNED ABOUT REFLECTION IN PROGRAMS

Because reflection was built into the activities of the programs described in this context, instances of reflection were prolific. However, the value of those instances differed markedly from teacher to teacher, and from one activity to another. This was particularly true given that reflection existed side by side with nonreflective goals and activities. The relationship between reflection and assessment caused noticeable friction. The discussion below highlights themes across the cases for an overall look at the effectiveness of reflection in programs of assessment and evaluation.

The Value of Structured Activity

Compared with their experiences with reflection in their daily school lives, the teachers identified significantly more instances of reflection that were both reflective and valuable in the contexts of the three programs. Why? Primarily, this difference stemmed from the value of structured activity.

Structured activities common to programs were more effective than more naturally occurring activities in achieving meaningful reflection. In many cases, the nature of the reflection called for by the programs was intense. Engaged in the rigors of thinking about practice, the teachers were thoroughly analytical and attentive to detail. Reflecting in this manner was highly valuable to the teachers when they felt challenged.

At the same time, the kind of intellectual, purposeful reflection encouraged by the programs evoked strong feelings from participants. They felt surprised (as when Underwood viewed his once-favorite lesson on videotape), satisfied (as when Green achieved "the perfect lesson"), and proud (as when Nichols delighted in learning from her student teacher). They could see the improvements in their teaching as their practice became aligned with standards, as they answered questions posed in the programs, and as they became clearer about their visions of good teaching. Even though the primary goal was often to satisfy an external assessor, the benefits of thinking about lessons, student learning, and the teaching philosophy served both students and teachers well. Consistently, the teachers agreed that their experiences with these programs for assessment were learning experiences, for rarely if ever were they asked to think so vigorously about their teaching outside the programs.

The Burden of Administrative Tasks

Despite the high level of effectiveness of program activities, a number of elements in the cases were also identified as neither reflective nor valuable.

Generally, these elements included activities that were most closely associated with the program requirements for organizing and administering the
activities, as in King's pilot evaluation program, or presentation of evidence, as in the written and videotaped evidence required by the National
Board. Such necessities overburdened the teachers and took precious time
away from reflection—an important point for those who would wish to
foster reflective practice in schools.

Teachers in Leadership Roles

One notable case in which a teacher didn't seem to be actively reflecting
in an activity—and yet found the activity valuable—was King's experience with her district's pilot teacher-assessment program. She played a
leadership role in this case, acting as a liaison between the district and the
school. She revealed her work in this capacity to be largely administrative
and explanatory as she brought teachers into the program. She viewed the
role as valuable nevertheless, because of the potential for the program to
eventually help teachers. Importantly for the focus of this book, the evaluation program she was leading focused heavily on reflection.

Similarly, the teachers held leadership roles as mentors. Both Green and
Nichols explained that working with teachers improved those teachers'
practice more than their own, whether they were mentoring other National
Board candidates, student teachers, or struggling colleagues. Again, this
was seen as significant, because when the teachers participating in the
study served as mentors, they were helping other teachers to reflect.

Reflection as Routine

When the teachers were not challenged by the activities or when they were
busy packaging the reflection for the sake of the external assessment, their
reflection became not only routine but fraught with frustration. At times,
the tedious tasks of organizing and verifying reflection became so overwhelming that the benefits of reflection were buried. When the teachers'
expertise matched or exceeded the demands of the tasks, the teachers focused more on the details of making their practice concrete for the sake of
assessment. The materials designed to support their reflective process—
standards booklets, directions, guidelines, software, questions—and even
colleagues became cumbersome if not completely obtrusive. At these

times, any benefit from the activities seemed only to serve the assessors or the program itself, and had little bearing on whether teachers learned from the process of reflecting.

How can the results of teachers' experiences in this context be useful in thinking about structuring reflection for teachers? In answering this question, it is helpful again to consider advantages and disadvantages of reflection as it occurred within programs.

Advantages of Reflection in the Programmatic Context

Having considered lessons from reflection in the context of programs, we now turn to a discussion of its advantages and disadvantages. The activities of the programs had significant advantages compared with those in the context of schools. Two key aspects were especially important: they were grounded in evidence and structured for reflection.

Grounded in evidence. Whether it started with a set of standards, a videotaped lesson, samples of student work, domains of teaching, or a lesson that a mentor teacher had observed, every case of reflection in this section was grounded in concrete evidence that became the object or starting point for reflection. Significantly, such evidence was linked closely to the teachers' experience in their own classrooms with the students and the subject they were teaching at the time. As discussed later in this book, this may be a very important difference in the activities the teachers valued versus those they did not.

Structured for reflection. By virtue of their embeddedness in programs, activities in this section were structured to help teachers succeed in reflecting. The process of the National Board, the framework of the pilot program, and even the recurring questions asked by cooperating teachers all guided teachers in moving beyond mere description of their work into more analytical, meaningful ways of thinking. Thus, the teachers were not only allowed to consider issues of teaching and learning in depth in a way not evident in the school context, but they were encouraged, even expected to do so.

Disadvantages of Reflection in the Programmatic Context

With the advantages noted above, reflection in the programmatic contexts can be said to be more effective than reflective in schools. But there were several disadvantages as well. Two items surfaced that were also seen in school-based reflection: time and culture. One more was added—the additional requirements of the programs.

Time for reflection. Given the time constraints felt by teachers during the regular school day, it was no surprise that heaping programs on at the end of those days was problematic. None of the programs were accompanied by available time during the day. As a result, the programs could be expected to succeed or fail based on the willingness of teachers to work on them in the evening and on weekends. Even mentoring conversations took place late in the day, long after the students had left and obligatory meetings had ended.

The cost of participation. Other "costs" associated with the programs— such as fees, emotional tolls, and professional risk—cannot be overlooked. In addition to time, these factors could easily become the basis upon which teachers decide if a program is "worth it." The pressures accompanying the programs, the voluntary aspect of participation, and the uniformity of the programs put the benefits of structured reflection at risk.

Culture. The teachers' participation in the programs bled into the school day, even though the programs weren't necessarily sponsored by the schools. Consequently, aspects of the school culture surfaced again in this context. Several examples surfaced in which the teachers' participation in the various programs was ignored, minimized, or rejected by fellow teachers and administrators. This was most obvious in Nichols's peer-mentoring arrangement, but also took place in a more subtle way when teachers showed by their absence of participation that they had not embraced King's district's pilot program and the National Board process. School culture was seen to work against reflection.

The advantages and disadvantages of programs for fostering reflection are important, for it is through such programs that teachers' reflection can be widely encouraged. However, as seen in the next section, other ways of supporting reflection approach the process differently and alleviate some of these challenges.

SUMMARY

Contexts for teacher assessment provided a unique opportunity for teachers to reflect, for they both encouraged reflection and provided the structure for reflective activities. The activities were consistently intellectual or academic in nature, compelling teachers to improve teaching and learning by using their minds well. This contrasted with activities in the school context, where teachers had to first create an environment for reflection, then choose among multiple matters for reflection, then structure their own reflective activities before thinking matters through without the support of an outside program or, for that matter, external standards for comparison.

Compared with the absent or unguided reflection that surfaced in schools, the kind of reflection present in these programs was generally more focused, more effective, and better designed to foster reflection. By design, teachers were asked questions that made them reflect on their practice. They believed the results impacted both teaching and learning. Importantly, however, such benefits were predicated on participation. Given the challenges accompanying the programs, such participation was hardly guaranteed.

This raises another question about reflection in teaching. What might be different if teachers could participate in structured activities to reflect on their practice *without* the pressures of assessment? Although examples were few and far between, the teachers did find opportunities to reflect in ways that suited them personally, with impressive results. These are the focus of the next section, which discusses examples of teachers reflecting on their own. In the next section, we see a contrast between the challenging, yet successful context for reflection and one that reaches teachers in a more personal, less stressful way. We now move from matters of the mind to matters of the heart.

Chapter Sixteen

Reflecting on One's Own:
The Personal Context

Why do teachers go into teaching? Ask many a veteran and you're bound to hear common replies. It's a calling. It's about the students. It's about creating a better world (Barth, 2001; Intrator, 2002). For most teachers, the job isn't primarily about schoolwide issues that are the focus of their everyday work life. It isn't about the intellectual challenges of teaching, so important in programs of teacher assessment. Rather, teaching is about human connection, contribution, and hope. It's about *heart*. In this section, the foundation for reflection is seen as deriving from the emotional commitment of the teacher. This section explores the essentials of reflection that go straight to the heart of the matter.

Cases from the contexts of schools and programs pose a troubling dilemma for incorporation of reflection into the lives of teachers. If reflection in schools can be inconsistent and unreliable, and reflection in programs of assessment strenuous and uncertain, what hope is there of sustaining reflective activities for teachers that are consistently meaningful? This section looks at teachers' personal approaches to reflection—on their own time, in their own ways. This is called the "personal context."

Each chapter in this section contains a description of the teachers' experiences with reflecting on their own. This chapter introduces teachers' general perspectives about reflection in these kinds of contexts. The next three chapters contain cases from contexts outside the typical parameters of a teacher's job not associated with particular programs of teacher assessment: a critical friends group, a mathematics conference, and a set of quiet, private spaces carved out by the teachers for their own thinking. The last chapter in the section discusses themes across the cases of teachers reflecting on their own.

A FRAMEWORK FOR LEARNING FROM THE CASES

What differentiates the personal context is the teachers' ownership of their reflective processes. In the contexts of schools and programs, the teachers were often seen engaging in reflection if and only if they believed it influenced teaching and learning; otherwise, they found ways of sidestepping or sabotaging activities that may or may not have been intended to be reflective, but that in either case struck the teachers as meaningless. In the personal context, when the teachers reflected on their own, their appreciation for the activities provided a dramatic contrast to their daily experiences in other contexts. What made these activities so engaging for the teachers? How could they inform efforts to design reflective activities for teachers? These are the overarching questions of this section.

To address these questions, we continue to examine cases of the teachers' experiences, using the four questions that have guided our discussion thus far:

1. Did reflection take place?
2. What supported or hindered reflection?
3. How was reflection valuable to teaching?
4. What can we learn from this case?

What we will find in addressing these questions is that reflection in the personal context, compared with the contexts of schools and programs, often inspired more enthusiasm on the part of the teachers, if not more learning and growth.

THE NATURE OF REFLECTION IN PERSONAL CONTEXTS

Compared with the nature of reflection in the schools and programs, reflection discussed in this section differed in notable ways. These differences centered on the personal side of activities and the importance of community, as discussed below.

The Personal Side of Reflection

The personal contexts in which teachers voluntarily chose to reflect on their practice differed from those of schools and programs. They were personal in a number of ways.

They were personal in that the teachers felt a sense of connection with the activities. In many cases, their reflection was associated with situations they enjoyed. For instance, Underwood found himself reflecting when he spent time with students as the swim team coach, senior class advisor, and hiking club supervisor. Much of Green's reflection occurred at a conference where she could collaborate with teachers as excited about math as she was. King enjoyed conversations with friends and family members who were also teachers—a process she found much more inviting and natural than filling out a chart to "show" her reflection. Nichols savored time with colleagues outside of school, in which ten teachers who she said would "never, ever connect" otherwise got together to reflect on their teaching. These activities satisfied sides of the teachers' personalities that were hidden in the other contexts, while also encouraging reflection.

"Personal" in this chapter also includes the notion of taking the whole teacher into account. Whereas other experiences tended to separate teachers into categories by department and subject matter, these experiences did not. The teachers could adjust the experience according to personal needs with respect to their unique teaching situations.

"Personal" in this chapter also acknowledges that the experiences honored the affective side of experience. There was a strong emotional current running throughout the activities discussed in this chapter that allowed people to feel connected, appreciated, trusted, and valued, even as the activities helped teachers reflect and learn. As Nichols put it, reflection in these contexts welcomed "the more human side" of teaching.

The Importance of Reflection and Community

Another difference in the teachers' experiences in this context compared with the others was an emphasis on community. Unlike with school- and program-based activities, in which the teachers' participation was obligatory (as when administrators required it) or was a means to an end (as with the National Board certification), their motivation for reflecting in personal contexts was tied to the relationships within a community. The importance teachers placed on these relationships was noteworthy, for it contributed to a deeper commitment to the activities and provided quite a contrast to the other contexts in which a sense of community was rarely nurtured, if it was present at all.

The idiosyncratic nature of the activities in this context made the teachers' experiences quite distinct in terms of content, structure, and relationship to reflection. Yet, each of the cases brought the teachers a sense of satisfaction and community.

SUMMARY

This section of the book features cases of the teachers' experiences with reflection in the contexts of their own personal choosing, each involving reflection as well as other valuable benefits, such as a personal sense of enjoyment and connection with a community. These contexts include a Critical Friends Group, a regional mathematics conference, and a set of quiet, private opportunities created by the teachers for their own thinking. We will ask questions about the cases, exploring their value in terms of reflection and beyond. We can expect to witness teachers' deep appreciation for these activities. The next chapter highlights a striking example of the personal context: a meeting of a critical friends group.

Chapter Seventeen

A Critical Friends Group

When does professional life end and personal life begin? Reflection is an iterative process that crosses both and may benefit from an integrated approach to thinking about teaching that invites time for personal fulfillment. One of the most successful formalized venues for fostering teachers' reflection does just that. In this chapter, we see reflection at work—and at play—in a critical friends group. The critical friends idea originated from the Coalition of Essential Schools. As described by Coalition materials: "A Critical Friends Group (CFG) brings together four to ten teachers within a school over at least two years, to help each other look seriously at their own classroom practice and make changes in it" (Coalition of Essential Schools, 2001). According to this definition, critical friends groups are designed to be reflective by providing an opportunity for teachers to look back on and learn from their practice in a collaborative community. With training and resources, groups of teachers are able to live up to the critical friends ideal. In this chapter, we visit such a group to see how reflection became infused in a highly personal, yet supremely professional experience. Two cases from this same group provide insight into how enriching reflection can be.

CASES FROM CRITICAL FRIENDS GROUPS

Of the four teachers, only Nichols belonged to a critical friends group. In the meeting of the critical friends group shown in the next case, reflection emerged immediately as teachers greeted each other on a school night. As the night went on, their reflection took on different forms according to changes in the activities and topics of conversations, running the gamut of topics important to teachers.

Case #1: The Critical Friends Protocol

One fall evening at Nichols's farmhouse, a close-knit group of teachers gathers for dinner. The smell of garlic wafts through the kitchen as teachers arrive, their arms full of dishes for the menu. The teachers hug and laugh. One dons an apron and starts his curry at the stove; another sets bread and cheese on the counter; everyone kicks off their shoes. Relaxing in the warmth of each other's company, they begin to talk about teaching. This is their critical friends group, a home for support, reflection, and connection.

The phases of the gathering correspond to the courses of the meal: casual debriefing of the day during appetizers, boisterous conversation over a sumptuous meal, and personal sharing after dinner. Finally, the structured part of the meeting takes place.

Just before the process begins, the ten teachers close their side conversations and settle quietly into their chairs at the dining room table—mindful, present, and ready to start. As the facilitator, Nichols reviews the protocol aloud, explaining that she will guide the conversation through several steps: A focus teacher will bring a lesson to the group, give a two-minute synopsis of the lesson, and state how it is she needs help. The group will then talk about the lesson, sharing opinions, offering critiques, raising questions, and making suggestions—all without the focus teacher's input. Following this, the focus person will have two minutes to clarify and say what she got out of the discussion.

Taking her cue, a teacher at the head of the table takes the floor. She is Greta, a woman with twenty-eight years' experience and the focus person of the evening.

To begin, Greta passes out copies of handouts for a lesson teaching writing to students learning English. "I feel like I'm pretty good at teaching reading, but I really struggle teaching writing," she tells the group. In this lesson, which she has recently taught, she wanted students to write personal narratives and enjoy the process—which they did, with the exception of a few students who she believed she had failed to reach with the assignment (as evidenced by substandard work). Looking back, she asks herself and the group, how could she help the students who didn't do well?

After Greta poses her question, Nichols restates it for the group and begins the discussion. The room fills with conversation. One teacher affirms the use of a rubric for grading and suggests using it as a set of standards to guide students from the beginning. Another suggests having students journal to explore topics. A third suggests having students write in their native language to increase confidence and comfort. The group brainstorms pre-writing activities to help students get ideas for topics, like telling stories out loud, drawing, and mind mapping. Every teacher at the table—including the newest member, the technology teacher, the facilitator, everyone—participates heartily by offering suggestions, discussing potential issues, and wondering aloud as they look for ways to inform Greta's puzzle of practice.

As the group discusses ideas for Greta's lesson, she takes notes on a small yellow pad. Finally, Nichols turns back to Greta. "Greta, why don't you tell us what you heard us say that will help you next time?" Greta reviews her notes aloud. She stars ideas, circles words, and says thoughtfully, "That's great. That's great." She thanks the group.

The protocol being completed, Greta gets up to whip the cream for dessert.

Debriefing the case. Of all the cases in this book, Nichols's critical friends group exemplifies the most successful reflection. Not only are the teachers engaged, interested, and having a great time, the structure of the protocol and the serious intent of the group make the meeting productive and move teaching forward.

Did reflection take place? This scenario presents all aspects of reflection: looking back on and learning from practice in an effort to continually improve. In this setting, reflecting was an integral part of the members' relationships.

The activity naturally had special advantages for the focus teacher. Greta's description of her lesson indicated that she had examined her own practice in advance of the meeting and put her finger on a particular problem. Resolving this problem, it seemed, could have positive implications for student learning. That she had this question on her mind suggested that she didn't feel able to resolve it by reflecting on her own, but the critical friends group provided some help.

What made this process especially noteworthy was that, now, nine teachers were all examining Greta's teaching and using their collective store of knowledge and skills to think about ways of improving the learning for students. Many of their ideas may easily have prompted silent and individualized reflection about their own practice in the minds of the participants, even as they helped Greta with hers.

What supported or hindered reflection? The most obvious component of this case is the protocol that structured the teachers' reflection. It had several elements:

- The focus teacher identified a puzzle of practice.
- She presented the puzzle to the group along with illustrative materials and a question.
- The facilitator restated the topic and clarified any misunderstanding.
- The group discussed the issue, using their own frames of reference.
- The focus person took notes as she listened and reported what she had learned.

This structure moved the teachers' thinking from challenge to resolution within the span of an hour, and the focus teacher left with new ideas about how to help her students learn.

According to Nichols, this process was designed to incorporate reflection in three ways. First, it involved looking back on practice as the focus teacher described her issue. Second, it involved learning in the midst of practice as the group discussed the lesson together. Third, it involved making informed and intelligent decisions about what to do and why as the focus teacher spoke again about what she had learned from the group. Thus, this one protocol incorporated all of the components of our definition of reflection.

But the protocol alone may not be sufficient to support such reflection. Nichols and her group members were quick to point out that the dynamics of this self-selected group, the trust among its members, and their mutual respect for each others' opinions allowed the protocol to be conducted with focus and purpose.

How was the reflection valuable to teaching? Greta wanted to help struggling students. Presented with the task of finding a lesson to present to the group, she chose one that had been otherwise successful, but hadn't reached a certain group of students. She isolated this problem in order to solve it, or at least to expand her repertoire in reaching the students being challenged most in her class. In her estimation, getting her colleagues' input on the issue was the only way to gain the new perspective that would help her support struggling students' learning. After the discussion, she seemed to be using the ideas from her colleagues to inform her practice on the spot. That the process had been valuable for her was suggested in her voice, her expression, and her words.

What can we learn from this case? As evidenced in the examples above, the critical friends group did reflect as planned, using the protocol Nichols described. As it turned out, the meeting revealed the group's capacity to sustain reflective conversation for long periods of time, even as they dined and relaxed in each other's company.

But even more striking than the reflection that took place was Nichols's overall perception of the group as valuable, apart from any specific activity. Nichols's appreciation for this group was palpable. Describing the critical friends group before the meeting, Nichols repeatedly praised the teachers and the community they had created. "I have really connected with those people. We've been at this three years. I've really, really connected with them. They are amazing young people. . . . I feel really fortunate to be able to work with them and learn from them." The tone in Nichols's voice as she spoke about these teachers could only be described as loving, suggesting that this group didn't just fill another slot on her schedule, but actually held a special place in her heart.

The protocol in this case was only part of a three-hour dinner. Interesting for a contrast is the conversation that took place afterward, when the teachers talked about teaching in an open forum over dessert. Reclining in their chairs, they savored their time and began to concentrate on a number of subjects for different durations and reasons—without seeming to have any specific agenda. We see the results in the next case.

Case #2: Conversations with Colleagues

When the critical friends group meeting is officially over, the best part of the meal finally begins. Dessert ushers in "oohs" and "aahs," as Greta makes her grand entrance back to the dining room with homemade cream puffs and little chocolate truffles. As she pours coffee from an old-fashioned pot, which she has brought especially for the occasion, the teachers settle into a serious conversation about the challenges of teaching.

The first topic raised is student tardiness. At first, the teachers just complain, swapping stories and describing the problem. Then the talk moves beyond description into the sharing of ideas. Philosophically, the teachers differ, and the school policy seems unclear, so they debate the topic on several points. Should tardiness affect academic grades? Should students be able to "work off" their tardies? Around the table, teachers show their sincere intent to learn. One leans across the table and asks her colleague to repeat a good idea: "Now, tell me, what do you do?" Another draws out more information from a colleague with a working system: "Tell me more about how you do that." In this way, the teachers listen to and learn from each other.

Other matters raised in the conversation seem harder to resolve. For instance, the teachers worry deeply about student participation in their classes, feeling discouraged about having to call on students who don't voluntarily participate in class. Although a few teachers suggest strategies for dealing with the issue, many seem to be contemplating the issue on a much deeper level, as evidenced by wrinkled brows and shaking heads. Some matters raised in the conversation seem altogether irresolvable. At one point, the teachers talk about the emotional toll of teaching and the heartbreak they always feel when students don't like their carefully planned lessons.

"This sucks," muttered a teacher, imitating a student.

Answered another: "It's a spear to the heart."

This reality of their vocation gives the teachers pause and seems almost out of the reach of reflection. Nodding seriously, they appear to find in each other, if not solutions, at least solace.

Returning to lighter topics, the teachers vent for a while about less pressing problems (such as the greasy food students were bringing to the classroom after lunch and student antics at school dances), but then just as easily, they switch back to more substantive topics, even taking on elusive matters that they believe undermine teaching, like grade inflation and students' resistance.

This topic hits a nerve with two teachers. One teacher is clearly fed up with students who "flatly refuse" to learn. She marvels at their surprise when they discover their grades are Fs. Expressing what she wants to say to these students, she yells, "Why shouldn't you have an F? You haven't done anything all quarter!" She angrily announces that 25% of their school's ninth and tenth graders have a D or below in English.

"Where has it become okay to do that?" Nichols bursts out with passion. But rather than dive deeper into the topic, her explosion is met with cynicism. Her colleague mimics what she sees as the public's perception of teachers, sneering sarcastically, "Well, you know, it's our fault."

At this remark, the conversation shuts down. After a heartbeat, someone raises a different issue and the conversation continues as before.

The rise and fall of questions and reflections lasts for an hour. The effectiveness of the discussion is apparent in the teachers' voices, the expressiveness of their faces and motions, the ring of their laughter, the heaviness of their sighs, their sense of urgency about teaching, and their general expression of confidence and expertise. Reflecting together not only seems to inform the teachers' practice, but it also seems to revitalize their commitment.

Debriefing the case. This case illustrates something rarely seen in other cases in this book: teachers talking about teaching with no overarching agenda. With no structure, no predetermined purpose, and seemingly all the time in the world, they illustrate reflection and learning in a form of their own.

Did reflection take place? The answer to this question is both yes and no. Like the informal collegial meetings of department members seen in an earlier chapter, this group specifically talked with an air of reflection— looking for questions, taking on issues, and addressing their concerns on a number of topics. Although the conversation wasn't necessarily designed to be a reflective opportunity (in fact, it wasn't "designed" at all), the teachers repeatedly initiated conversation that invited and encouraged reflection on teaching. The dialogue moved freely from storytelling to the daily matters of teaching to critical issues.

Whether the conversation could fairly be called "reflective" depended on the moment, however. The discussion about tardiness moved the teachers from their present levels of awareness to ideas and understanding, as they exchanged ideas and learned from each other. But momentary complaints about greasy food and computer glitches merely floated through the conversation briefly. Yet, every one of the topics raised for discussion carried the potential to spark reflection in the minds of the teachers. Despite the ebb and flow of actual reflection throughout the discussion, the teachers generally maintained a reflective stance as they followed the rhythms of conversation.

Only once did a topic expose the apparent limit of their reflective capacity. When Nichols's outburst pinned down a major societal issue—student apathy and resistance to learning—the teachers seemed positively stumped. Although her question struck at a vital problem for teachers and could have opened the door for deepest discussions about why and how students fail, the teachers seemed to lack the ability to follow through. The reflective moment was lost and the opportunity to address Nichols's critical question was missed.

What supported or hindered reflection? As in the previous case, the teachers drew on the closeness of the group in generating this level of conversation. Trust, familiarity, and a genuine concern for teaching and each other motivated them to take the topics seriously and reflect through them together.

This part of the meeting, however, lacked structure altogether. This was both a strength and a weakness in terms of reflection. On the positive side, the open forum format allowed the teachers to raise any topic on their minds, explore it in a number of ways, and stay with it until the discussion felt complete. On the negative side, this approach produced an uneven quality of reflection. The teachers most frequently described what they were doing; only sometimes compared ideas in a way that could enhance teaching and learning; and could only raise but not address the most critical issues they faced. Without a structure to guide them into the deepest levels of reflection, they seemed to lack the skills or strategies to tackle the hardest questions.

How was the reflection valuable to teaching? In this form of reflection, the teachers explored problems, ideas, and options in a way that could inform their own practice and thinking. They engaged with the most mundane of topics—such as tardiness and grading software—from different angles that allowed the conversation to flow in interesting, humorous, serious, light-hearted, practical, and philosophical directions. Not one of the teachers looked disengaged, disinterested, or distracted, suggesting by their frowns, nods, and exclamations that they found the conversation meaningful.

For Nichols, the value of this group was almost beyond description. In response to a comment about her critical friends group ("It sounds like yours is a very successful one!"), she responded, "Oh, my God, you have no idea." Her colleagues seemed to agree when they spoke of their experience with the group. Asserting her perception of the group's importance in their work, one of the teachers stated, "At some point, this has really helped us all." Around the table, the rest of the teachers nodded in unison. These "critical friends," assembled for the purpose of reflection, said they reaped even more than was sown, harvesting friendship, support, safety, and reassurance along with their learning.

What can we learn from this case? The case is perhaps most valuable for illustrating what reflection can add to teaching when teachers lead their own way. With the combination of skills from the critical friends model, a long-term collaborative relationship, and the freedom to talk as they chose, these teachers became more energetic about reflecting on teaching than teachers in almost any other context in this book. Perhaps in some cases the most valuable approach to fostering reflection is to give teachers the tools and the time to do it, and then to step out of the way.

SUMMARY

Overall, Nichols's critical friends group exemplified valuable reflection. Together, the members exhibited thoughtfulness and an extraordinary capacity to think about teaching on a number of levels, from sharing to deliberating to contemplating philosophical issues. With the support of their protocol, the guidance of a talented facilitator, and a culture of trust, the teachers grappled with difficult questions. The apparently effortless succession of ideas flowed from the needs of the teachers as they raised them spontaneously in the safety of the group, while a sound foundation of collegiality and friendship appeared to uphold the quality of the discussion. Reflection thrived in the connection in the meeting between the critical friends who gathered for a shared meal in a comfortable home—symbols of wholeness and well-being, nourishment and nurturance, trust and connection.

But the mutual affection in the group seemed even more important to Nichols than the opportunity to reflect on practice. In a profession she called "isolated," Nichols loved the experience of connecting with colleagues who would "never, ever" otherwise connect. Speaking of the other teachers in the group, Nichols said, "They're fabulous. They're amazing. Amazing." She believed the rest of the group would agree. "They don't ever miss. They love doing it." In an element often overlooked in school-based and program-based activities, these teachers welcomed and prioritized emotion and affection as an aspect of success. In thinking and talking about their roles as teachers, they communicated to each other with genuine respect and an appreciation they said was seldom expressed in their profession—and one that, for them, was the heart of the experience.

The next chapter continues with this theme of community in teacher-selected activities. This time, we witness Green's experience with reflection in one of her favorite events of the year: an annual mathematics conference.

Chapter Eighteen

A Regional Conference

Are teachers more open to reflection when the topic connects to their passion? We can glimpse the power of personal interest in generating reflection by following a teacher into an experience in which her passion is ignited: a professional conference. Although also a venue for reflection, in contrast to the home-centered critical friends group, conferences take teachers away from their school contexts and join them with other professionals in interest-based groups. Elements of personal interaction and subject matter fascination combine for the makings of reflection. Since conferences provide the opportunity to connect with other professionals in the field and gather new information to inform practice, they would seem to be events with potential opportunities for reflection.

Attending conferences was a popular activity for all of the teachers, who reported regularly presenting at conferences, whether they were associated with subject matter areas (like Green's mathematics conferences), student populations (like the conferences on gifted learning attended by King and Nichols), or associations (like the National Education Association meeting attended by Underwood). In this chapter, we witness one teacher's experiences in three cases drawn from a single conference that sparked reflection and excitement in ways she rarely experienced at school.

CASES FROM A REGIONAL CONFERENCE

One teacher's experience provides the cases in this chapter. Green regularly attends an annual regional mathematics conference. Her recent experience, held at a luxurious historic hotel far from her home, was a high point of her year. "I've attended them every year since I've started teaching," she declared. "It's the best thing you can ever do!" To Green, the experience was positively invaluable. She said, "I can't imagine not going to a math conference. . . . It's just terribly beneficial." The value Green placed on her attendance at the conference was evident in these comments; it was also evident in the effort she expended to get herself there. Because of a shortage of substitute teachers, Green had some difficulty managing to attend. With some finagling and persuasion, however, she was able to make arrangements for the conference.

The cases below describe Green's weekend at the conference. Like the critical friends group for Nichols, the regional mathematics conference was an experience Green treasured. Also like the critical friends group, nearly the entire experience had the potential to be reflective. In Green's reports, many of the activities were reflective; those that weren't were nevertheless important for other reasons. Her descriptions of the activities included a variety of opportunities, from conference sessions to professional connections to fun and the lighter side of learning, which is always part of the experience.

Case #1: A Conference Session

In her math classes, Green has always valued a sense of community. One of the things she loves to do is celebrate students' birthdays. "I collect birthdays every year at the beginning of school and I keep them on my desk calendar, and my students bring goodies on their birthday. And they do! It's great!" To tie the celebrations into mathematics, Green amazes students by correctly predicting that two of them will have the same birthday. She is always right. "How?" they want to know. She then explains to them what she calls "the birthday problem"—a mathematical probability that "If there [are] over twenty-three people in the room, two of you will have the same birthday."

Despite this mathematical connection, Green emphasizes the celebration aspect of birthdays over the mathematics. In fact, the mathematical part of the birthday celebrations is minimal, because the "birthday problem" is so difficult to explain. "Probability can get very complicated, and you can't just teach it to anybody without the probability background . . .

because it normally requires combinations and permutations of factorials." Green typically tells her classes about this probability without actually teaching the concepts. However, a conference session provides a chance to do more.

In the session, a presenter shows teachers how to think about the probability behind the birthday problem in a manner appropriate for an algebra class using "fractions instead of complicated math." Green immediately realizes that this can make the concept behind the birthday problem accessible to students in the less-advanced math classes. Although Green has always understood the concept, she leaves knowing for the first time how to explain it to students. From now on, she plans to incorporate it into the existing birthday activities in her classroom—advancing her practice from superficially explaining probability to students to actually helping them learn it as they celebrate each others' birthdays.

Debriefing the case. At the conference, the session Green attended helped her advance her teaching practice by helping her learn new ways of thinking about teaching strategies she was already using. She identified this process of incorporating new knowledge into her thinking as a valuable and reflective component of the conference.

Did reflection take place? For Green, the answer to this question is certainly yes. The new information Green gained from the presenter provided the opportunity for Green to reflect in, on, and for practice as she incorporated the new ideas into her previously designed lessons. This kind of reflection created a meaningful experience when she made the effort to improve her practice and tie celebratory occasions to subject-matter content.

Interestingly, Green's description of other sessions included fun mathematical activities that teachers could easily adopt whole cloth in a rather nonreflective way of improving practice. Such sessions can be seen as giving teachers lessons without expecting them to understand the conceptual underpinnings—a common criticism of such sessions. In a profession sometimes accused of being saturated with unsubstantial "cool" or fun activities, it is important to note that Green did, in fact, reflect on the activities she received at conferences once she returned to her school. In several observations of her classroom teaching, it was apparent that Green used fun activities to teach mathematics and that she also had done the kind of reflection necessary to incorporate the lessons for meaningful learning and had not just imported them from conferences.

What supported or hindered reflection? Both Green and the conference presenter can be credited with supporting reflection in this case. The conference session provided Green with a sense of what the activity had to offer mathematically, but her own reflection gave her the tools to understand when to use it and why. Reflection can be built into the session by asking teachers questions directly, such as, "How can you use this information to adapt lessons you already teach?" "In what classes would you use this information, when, and why?" and "How does this session connect with the content you already teach in your classes?" To do so would be to prompt teachers explicitly to do what came so naturally to Green.

How was the reflection valuable to teaching? Green's students always enjoyed the birthday celebrations. But as one of her signature teaching characteristics, Green rarely did anything in class that wasn't somehow connected to math. The reflection that occurred as a result of the session strengthened her celebration in a way that had learning value for students, even as she nurtured the community in her classroom.

What can we learn from this case? This case reveals the private side of learning. Green had to struggle to get to the conference—a suggestion that such conferences are seen as peripheral to teacher development, a perk available only when excess money is available. But Green's learning, even in this one short session, shows that such conferences can spark important reflection that actually improves teaching and learning.

The mathematics conference drew together people of similar interests and fields; not surprisingly, Green had the opportunity to meet like-minded people, as seen in the next case. Many of her conversations with people at the conference were nonreflective—just as conversations with colleagues could be nonreflective in school contexts and in the critical friends group. But unlike other nonreflective conversations, which the teachers indicated made little difference to teaching and learning, these conversations generated new connections and strengthened a network that kept Green active in her profession. Thus they provided informative illustrations about the kinds of conversations that might be important to create in reflective activities for teachers.

Case #2: Conversations with Colleagues

On this trip to the conference, Green spends plenty of time connecting and reconnecting with friends, teachers, and others who share her interest in mathematics. Starting with the ride up on the ferry, Green and the colleagues she has encouraged to come to the conference talk for hours about lots of things and about nothing in particular. At the conference, Green meets a conference organizer from the National Council of Teachers of Mathematics, resulting in an opportunity for Green to present at an upcoming conference. She also meets a teacher who can help Green with a grant she is writing and a textbook distributor who agrees to help fund one of Green's professional groups. Throughout the conference, Green runs into people she's known for years, including her master's program adviser, the parent of one of her students, and two of her college professors. Each of the conversations takes place in a pleasant, relaxed environment: while traveling, over lunch, and even during a wine-and-cheese reception. Green moves from one event to another, meeting new people and renewing lasting relationships with others interested, as she is, in advancing the teaching of mathematics.

Debriefing the case. Green's conversations with colleagues overviewed here, such a big part of the conference for Green, serve as an interesting contrast to other types of conversations with colleagues described throughout this book. Reflective or otherwise, these conversations were valuable to Green, making them of interest for those structuring activities for teachers that are valuable enough to motivate teacher participation in the conferences.

Did reflection take place? Nothing in Green's recounting of these conversations signified them as reflective. In many ways, reflection seemed absent. Nevertheless, the conversations were meaningful and filled an important role in Green's professional life. Moreover, they had the potential to benefit the profession, for professions advance with the generation of knowledge and skills shared by people like Green.

What supported or hindered reflection? Details about Green's conversations with her colleagues provide clues to their nature and their ability to support or hinder reflection. We know from witnessing conversations in Nichols's critical friends groups and Underwood's department, for example, that when teachers of similar interests, who place similar importance on teaching, and who respect each others' opinions, come together, the occurrence of reflection is likely. It is welcome and the teachers have the time and the opportunity to explore issues, questions, and ideas with each other—unlike in most staff meetings and department meetings and even in preparing for the National Board.

However, we also know that such open-ended, unstructured conversations can limit reflective expression. This has been true in other cases when one teacher in a group just wanted to complain, hampering other teachers' efforts to reflect productively in order to find new ideas. It has also been true when the topic of conversation seemed outside of teachers' control. Reflecting on such issues often requires more support, in the form of guiding questions and activities such as those seen in programs of teacher assessment.

All of this is to say that Green's conversations may or may not have involved reflection. The interesting question to ask, then, is whether such conversations are valuable enough to teachers to recognize them as legitimate professional activity.

How was the reflection valuable to teaching? Overall, the conversations Green held at the conference were primarily valuable to her as a member of the profession. Important (if often overlooked) elements of teaching, professional advancement and renewal contribute significantly to teachers' effectiveness in the classroom. In fact, involvement in one's profession and an ability to connect professional activities to student learning are critical attributes of accomplished teachers as defined by the National Board—the most highly recognized assessor of teaching quality. Whether or not reflection took place in these conversations, they contributed to Green's growth as a teacher, with positive influences on her students.

Green's enthusiasm in telling the stories, the eagerness in her eyes, and the delight in her voice at having made these connections suggested that making them was an important and valuable experience that wouldn't have taken place if not for the conference. This kind of emotional response—so different from embittered accounts of frustration in, for example, department meetings and unsuccessful mentoring relationships—suggested that designers of reflective activities would do well to learn about what created such positive results in successful conversations among teachers, even when they weren't reflective.

What can we learn from this case? Again, Green didn't see these conversations as particularly reflective. She did, however, describe them as consistently meaningful. The real value in these connections was strengthening a network within which reflection could take place—the very feature missing in Green's school. Asked if there were other times outside of conferences when she could have such conversations with colleagues, she spat out, "No." But at the conference, Green and her colleagues "shared the things we learned and what we do in our classroom." According to her, Green was able to find this opportunity for collegial reflection only away from school, at the conference.

Some of the conference sessions, as seen in the next case, served to excite and inspire teachers. Again, these sessions had a rather loose relationship to reflection, but Green's telling of the experiences revealed them to be quite meaningful and showed her learning about mathematics in a way that directly impacted her teaching. Thus, they offered important information about meaningful activities in general that would also be useful in structuring reflective activities for teachers.

Case #3: Fun and the Lighter Side of Learning

At the end of the conference, a few of the sessions stand out as inspiring to Green. In the keynote session, the presenter exhibited works of art related to mathematics: "He showed us sculptures on the east coast that are just tiles. Different colors of tiles. It looks like it's just this messy mosaic. But the tiles are laid out in the Fibonacci sequence. One, one, two, three, five, eight, thirteen." The presenter showed another mosaic in which each tile represented a number; this time the seemingly aimless pattern was laid out in the order of pi. The presenter also brought along records to entertain the audience, each with mathematics-related words in the title. Thinking back on this part of the session, Green exclaims enthusiastically, "It was fun!"

A similar situation took place in the closing session, which Green describes as "just wonderful," "dynamic," and "uplifting." This time, the presenter directly initiated reflection by asking a single question of his audience filled with teachers on their way back to school after a conference: "Why do things differently?" He then modeled mathematics teaching while entertaining the teachers. He engaged the teachers in fun math problems, showed them how to teach math in context, and encouraged reflection by asking teachers to be thoughtful about what they were doing and why.

The serendipitous high point of the conference came at the end, when Green won a door prize for her colleague. This teacher, attending the conference for the first time, had gone to a workshop on algebra blocks. Green recalls, "She'd never used them before, and she was so excited." Tickled to have won a prize, Green ran up to get it and received a set of algebra blocks! Her delight was irrepressible. "I won them! So I said, 'Yay!' And I ran down and brought them back to her. She was so excited. I said, 'Look, they're for you!'" In an event consistent with the rest of the conference, this purely playful moment left Green feeling inspired, revived, and enthusiastic.

Debriefing the case. As was true in the critical friends group, not every moment of the conference sessions was reflective. However, every moment Green described about her conference experience was in some way significant to her. These moments engendered such positive emotions that they stand out as unique among the experiences of all four teachers described throughout the book.

Did reflection take place? In the examples from the case, some of the most exciting sessions Green described didn't encourage reflection. She nevertheless seemed inspired by the session and expressed an excitement and appreciation for the experience that rarely arose in other experiences described by teachers in the study across all three contexts. Thus, these essentially nonreflective sessions—seemingly irrelevant in a book about reflection—actually reached the "whole teacher" in a way few other experiences did and stood out for her as memorable and meaningful.

Only one of the three sessions (the closing session) explicitly invited reflection. But Green didn't emphasize the reflective aspect of the talk as being the most important. The entertaining presentation of mathematics and the fun she had as a participant in the session also made it stand out in her mind. She saw the session as a valuable experience to her for many reasons, including reflection. This provides a significant contrast to other cases in this book, in which reflective activities were often either (1) effective but focused, intense, and challenging (as seen in the National Board process) or (2) ineffective and of little interest to teachers, despite a single focus on reflection (as seen in department meetings with so-called reflective charts to fill out). The closing session from Green's conference illustrates one way in which a conference presenter was able to support reflection while also inspiring teachers in an enjoyable and engaging way.

The admittedly nonreflective high note on which this conference ended provided dramatic contrast to the often tedious, even frustrating, nonreflective experiences in the programmatic contexts and contrasts even more strikingly with the nonreflective experiences in the school setting that caused protests, bitterness, and resentment. Compared with these kinds of experiences that so obviously reached teachers like Green on a personal level, it doesn't seem at all surprising that the teachers expressed far less enthusiasm for dry activities that characterized professional and programmatic opportunities for reflection.

What supported or hindered reflection? The three sessions highlighted in this case make a clear point for reflection: it is most likely to occur when it is explicitly prompted. We know from other cases that *simply* prompting reflection may not make it occur. And yet, combined with a context that interests teachers and motivates them to think about improving their practice, asking a reflective question as in the closing session described in the case ("Why do things differently?") may be enough to leave teachers pondering their practice and preparing to make positive changes.

How was the reflection valuable to teaching? As illustrated in the examples in the case, Green believed the conference sustained her ability to make informed and intelligent decisions about practice by staying current. No doubt, two of the three sessions Green described could be considered "merely" fun or simply technical; certainly it would be possible for teachers to attend them without reflecting on their practice. As was true for Nichols's critical friends group, Green's conference provided the opportunity for reflection and only occasionally explicitly encouraged it. This being the case, the success of the activities and the realization of their reflective potential depended on Green's personal decision to engage in reflection—a decision less frequently seen by other teachers in other opportunities and in other contexts.

What can we learn from this case? This case is included in this chapter as a way of highlighting some of the important aspects of conferences, even some that are minimally reflective. The kinds of benefits Green received from the lighter side of the conference included a renewed sense of enthusiasm for mathematics, teaching, and involvement in her profession. Each of these separately contributes to reflection, for only when teachers are actively engaged in their work are they likely to care enough to be their very best. When reflection is built into more typical teaching activities—such as staff meetings and teacher evaluation—activity planners would do well to also build in a sense of camaraderie, excitement, and inspiration.

SUMMARY

As described by Green, her experiences over the course of a conference weekend were sometimes reflective and, in her mind, consistently valuable. She learned in the midst of the sessions, looked back on her lessons and considered how to improve them, and looked ahead to her future units with a fresh store of ideas to inform her practice. The nonreflective events were also important to Green, for various reasons.

Of all of her professional activities (and there were many), attending conferences was one Green wholeheartedly defended. For her, the advantages of conferences exceeded practical knowledge. Green didn't just take the activities whole cloth and insert them into her courses; as she described her process, she integrated new ideas with the needs of her students and the concepts of the curriculum to improve student learning about mathematics.

Other benefits of the conference were distinctly emotional—an element of teaching typically absent from the teachers' descriptions throughout this study.

Not only [do] I always get things I can use in my class. Always. But also, you feel good when you come back. Because you're there with all these other energetic math teachers who are just as excited and interested in math as you are, instead of working in your building where you don't feel supported. . . . You always come back excited from a math conference for the next several months.

Green's spirited retelling of conference stories compared with a rather disgruntled attitude about her school underscored the role of personal fulfillment in reflection and teaching.

Although Green's opinion of conferences was so high, they were threatened by a shortage of resources (i.e., substitutes and funds). The lack of resources jeopardized Green's future at conferences, especially given the increasing difficulty of getting time off to attend. But Green's passion seemed to have a way of outsmarting the policies, and she had every intention of continuing her learning, despite the difficulties she faced. Knowing the benefits of conferences, she said she refused to follow what she saw as a nonreflective norm among teachers—to "never go and never do anything different in their classroom. That happens all the time."

For their part, she and the other three teachers in this study often did things differently as a result of their reflection. This is the subject of the next chapter, which contains cases of teachers reflecting in quiet spaces and personal places carved out just for the purpose.

Chapter Nineteen

Quiet Spaces and Personal Places

We've seen reflection throughout this book as alternatingly challenging, frustrating, thrilling, fun, inspiring, and laborious. What about the images of reflection as serene, contemplative, and private? Unlike in many of the activities in this book, reflection does indeed take place in the quiet spaces teachers carve out for personal time. Regardless of their physical location—in a classroom, at home, at a meeting, or on an afternoon jog— teachers may retreat to personal places in their minds, where they find a separate space to reflect. The three cases in this chapter showcase these activities. Involving reading, writing, and thinking, these examples show reflection as a way of life.

CASES FROM TEACHERS' INDIVIDUALIZED ACTIVITIES

In the first case, involving reflection at home, King described how the dreary thought of lesson planning developed into a thoughtful time to read and reflect.

Case #1: Reading

Arriving home after dinner at a friend's house late on a Sunday evening, King regretfully sits down to work. Despite the late hour, she plunks herself down to read an article, "Theories of Critical Election," for a government class she is teaching the next day. Her husband, also a teacher, spots her reading and asks to see the article. Before long, the two are reading the article aloud in sections. King's husband reads the first two pages, then together they stop and mull it over. King considers which points will most interest students and make the point she wants the lesson to make. King reads the next two pages and they stop and talk it over again. Again, they consider how to use the information with students. Before long, they have read the entire article, even taking time to examine the illustrations. What started as a laborious effort to work ends as a thoughtful, collaborative reading that has brought King new ideas for teaching her class.

Debriefing the case. King's demeanor as she described this night reflected her feelings about the event. In a soft, casual voice, she reported, "It was totally impromptu. . . . It was a chance to reflect on that [article] with an audience. I was really delighted, actually. It worked very nicely for me." This description highlighted two features of reflection common in this context—the importance of a partner with whom to reflect and the role of affect in making experiences seem valuable on a personal, not just professional, level.

Did reflection take place? King raised this example as a kind of reflection typical of her behind-the-scenes teaching. An avid reader, she often reflected on articles and other material as a way of staying on top of her subject matter and bringing current events to her students. Simply reading wasn't the impact; *reflecting* on the reading helped her make it relevant to students.

What supported or hindered reflection? King's husband played a critical role in this particular example of reading. Having such a partner—be it a family member, a colleague, or a professional study group—is often recognized as fruitful for learning from reading. For many teachers, such opportunities are lacking. Yet, King's case serves as a reminder that reading new information can be vital to initiating reflection.

How was the reflection valuable to teaching? Accomplished teachers, again as defined by the National Board for Professional Teaching Standards, stay current in their fields. King, one year away from retirement, could easily have taught social studies without ever increasing her knowledge. Yet, a single day in her classroom reveals that she teaches at the cutting edge of her field, bringing in examples from real-world events and the most contemporary thinking on politics, government, and history. In a world of change, that teachers to read and reflect for the sake of improving their practice is vital.

What can we learn from this case? Teachers are rarely seen reading. Grading papers, talking to students, teaching classes, attending meetings, and endless other activities fill their days from before students arrive until they leave. This case provides a peek into the life of a teacher in the other hours of the day, as she reflects on her subject and her practice. It serves as a reminder that some of the most essential elements of teaching are the least evident to the public. For King, this spontaneous chance to think aloud with her husband was a reflective event she found both personally and professionally valuable.

Similar to reading, writing is an activity that teachers engage in when few people see them at work. In the next case, we see how writing informs Nichols's daily instruction and her continual thinking about teaching.

Case #2: Writing

A black-and-white composition book sits discreetly on Nichols's front desk. Hidden under stacks of student papers, grade books, and memos, it almost appears unimportant. But when Nichols describes how she reflects on her practice, she pulls it out directly, showing she knows exactly where it is.

The book is chock-full of Nichols's bold cursive in entries from one to several paragraphs long. In it, she collects notes, reminders, thoughts, and miscellaneous "reflections" on her experiences throughout the days and over the years. She even writes on the journal topics she gives students—including the topic she has given her sixth period today: "What's important to me everyday?" Just an hour before, Nichols could be seen earnestly answering the question as her students wrote theirs at their desks.

Reflecting by writing is a habit for Nichols—one of the main ways she makes sense of her practice. She explains, "I keep a journal to reflect on what's gone on with my day or my week or my month." One of Nichols's main uses for the journal is to reflect on troubling issues of teaching. For instance, if she is struggling with a student, she writes about the issue in the book. She then sits with it awhile, thinking about the issue over a period of a few days or weeks. Then she returns to the journal, reads what she's written, and writes her way into a new perspective. In this way, Nichols brings clarity to her thoughts and works through issues that confront teachers every day.

Other topics also get attention in the journal, including reflections on parent conferences, ideas that come from conferences and meetings she attends, and interactions with colleagues. In short, Nichols's trusty "book," as she calls it, helps her think through all aspects of her teaching in a way she finds natural and indispensable.

Debriefing the case. As in the previous case, this case reveals a side to teaching little known to students, fellow teachers, and administrators. Nichols and teachers like her use writing as a medium for reflection—one that requires quiet time often long after the end of the day.

Did reflection take place? As we've seen in teachers' self-structured reflective activities elsewhere, Nichols's entries might have just as easily been nonreflective as reflective. But the fact that Nichols engaged in personal writing meant that the opportunities to initiate reflection for herself at least existed—something not always true in other contexts. Even though it seemed likely that her journal might not always contain writing that could be called reflection, her description of the way she used journals indicated otherwise. For her, writing *was* her reflection: a way to look deeply into all elements of practice for the purpose of improving her teaching.

What supported or hindered reflection? What Nichols liked about her system implied it adapted to her needs instead of the other way around: "It's all in one place. I'm getting too old to remember different places. So . . . this [book] has got lots of different things in it." In her personal journal, Nichols was able to reflect on anything and everything that struck her as important, whenever she found it valuable to do so. This illustrates the extreme opposite of reflective experiences described in other chapters that narrowed the focus to matters on a specific agenda or predetermined framework, with little regard to the personal side of teachers' experience.

How was the reflection valuable to teaching? Only by watching Nichols in action can one fully appreciate the impact of her reflection on students. In the most challenging moments with students, parents, and faculty, Nichols was thoughtful, humble, and effective—often saying, "Let me think about that and get back to you." In her hectic day, Nichols found a way to pause in a situation, look it over thoroughly in writing, and return to it when she was ready. Continual accolades from the people who knew her testified that her approach made her an exemplary teacher.

The spaces teachers made for their private thoughts and reflections could take place almost anytime, anywhere. Another teacher, Underwood, described an experience that signified the importance of solitary time for the opportunity to think and reflect, as we see in the next case.

Case #3: Thinking

An adviser to the hiking club, a union member, and the coach of the swim team, Underwood is involved in a number of activities that interest him personally and involve him with students. These activities play an important part in his life as a teacher. As he says, "The things I like most about teaching probably have nothing to do with my content area at all." And yet, his activities can be taxing as well as sustaining.

Underwood reflects on this in the down time between races at a swim meet. In his solitary time between races, he has plenty of time to think alone by the pool. What he thinks about is participating in coaching.

> *Coaching swimming is starting to wear me down, and I'm starting to wonder. . . . I know I'm not doing as good a job at coaching as I did ten years ago. Part of it is because it's harder to do as good a job, because of all the paperwork and administrative tasks. I'm less willing to do the paperwork. When I started, I would have considered it to be part of my job, but they keep adding to it. Now I start to think it's a needless part of my job, and it detracts from what I'm doing.*

Essentially, Underwood wonders in his reflection if he is being the coach he wants to be—and if he even can be anymore.

Underwood's private reflection also incorporates other aspects of his life unrelated to teaching: he is getting married and wants more personal time. "I don't know if as a newlywed . . . I want to be working sixty hours," he thinks to himself. Again, Underwood's reflection raises difficult personal questions that intersect with his professional life. In the stretches of time where he doesn't teach or coach, Underwood is taking the chance to think deeply about what he wants from his teaching and how he is willing to contribute as his life changes in significant ways.

Debriefing the case. Like the other cases in this chapter, Underwood's reflection moved beyond the realm of teaching and incorporated other aspects of his life. Underwood's feelings about his time may seem unrelated to reflective practice, but to him, they were big parts of his life that had bearing on his career. In the personal space created by the extra time during the swim meet, Underwood found the conditions he needed to do some thinking about how the different parts of his personal and professional lives were interacting.

Did reflection take place? Although he did not arrive at a conclusion, Underwood's thinking had bearing on his work. He was not reflecting on teaching, but on whether he could continue to coach and teach at all. In the most personal sense, his reflection was a way of discovering what he was doing and why—in general as well as in the classroom.

What supported or hindered reflection? In a jam-packed schedule, having down time supported Underwood's reflection the most. His case makes the point that in the absence of time and structured guidelines, reflection nevertheless takes place.

How was reflection valuable to teaching? Underwood's case is weakest on this point: one might wonder how his personal choices to coach and teach would ever affect his students. But Underwood was a beloved coach and distinguished teacher with much to offer his students. His reflection on his professional role links to a much bigger issue: the teacher shortage looming in this nation. As some educators argue (Intrator, 2002; Palmer, 1997, 1998), there is no more important subject for reflection than the identity and integrity of the teacher upon whom all good teaching rests.

What can we learn from this case? As in previous cases, this case shows reflection taking place in ways few can see. The fundamental importance of Underwood's reflection underscores the depth to which it can go and shows it to be valuable whenever and wherever it can occur, even on one's own by the side of the pool.

SUMMARY

Unlike more structured types of reflection, the reflective activities described above seemed to come more naturally to these teachers, arising from the opportunities in daily life, as opposed to the organized activities in critical friends meetings and conferences. Reading, talking, writing, and thinking were inexpensive, independent, enjoyable, accessible activities in which teachers engaged for the sake of interest, well outside the boundaries of their professional responsibilities and the structured support of programs. Admittedly, these tended to be less rigorous than other forms of reflection. They were also less informed by external sources and alternative perspectives that were so important in other valuable experiences. However, because the teachers valued them so highly, the cases in this chapter also illustrated ways that reflection happened without the kinds of coercion and stress sometimes apparent in other activities. Sometimes, these activities were merely social, but more often than not they also informed the teachers' practice. Whether the activities were reflective or not, the teachers found them significant, often leaving them with a sense of personal fulfillment—a cue for those who would like to create valuable reflective experiences for teachers.

We have seen several cases of teachers reflecting on their own: in a critical friends group, at a conference, and in a set of places reserved for private reflection. The next chapter discusses themes across these cases and their value in supporting reflection.

Chapter Twenty

The Conditions for
Reflecting on One's Own

REVIEW OF THE SECTION: THE CONDITIONS
FOR REFLECTING ON ONE'S OWN

The cases included in this section didn't come from school-based goals and concerns, as seen in the professional context. Nor did they respond to programs designed to support quality teaching, as seen in the programmatic context. Reflection in personal contexts emerged from the intentions of the teachers. The activities didn't just encourage reflection, they actually encouraged the heart (Kouzes & Posner, 1999).

In this way, they provided quite a contrast to other cases in this book. Unlike the uninspiring meetings and the tedious tasks seen in other contexts, every single one of this section's cases was considered valuable by the teachers. Also unlike the experiences in other contexts, the activities took place on the teachers' own time and were associated with a number of important benefits. Whether they were participating in a critical friends group, a conference, or some private activity, the teachers found a sense of fulfillment in their reflection in these cases. However, despite the teachers' unfettered enthusiasm for these experiences, a close look also revealed some noteworthy challenges.

This chapter discusses themes throughout the cases in this section that shed light on how reflection occurred in the contexts teachers created for themselves when reflecting on their own time, in their own ways. The first part of this chapter discusses the place of reflection in these contexts as compared with its place in schools or programs of teacher assessment. It also discusses the challenges and benefits of reflection in this context. The next part discusses lessons learned from the cases and advantages and disadvantages of teacher choice as a way of encouraging reflective practice.

The Place of Reflection by Choice

Of all the cases in this section, only two were specially designed by others to encourage and support reflection: the critical friends group protocol and the closing session of the mathematics conference. The other reflective events took place simply when and where the teachers made room for them, according to their individual and personal preferences. The fact that they engaged in these activities in the evenings, at home, on weekends, and even during vacations signified the activities were a priority in their lives, even though they weren't a priority for their schools. Reflection took place *even when it wasn't structured* for them; the teachers took up the responsibility for thinking about practice on their own in some impressively productive ways.

However, the freedom came with a price. Reflective activities in personal context occurred sporadically. Underwood's reflection during his coaching and advising took place after school, during the late afternoons, evenings, and weekends throughout the year, including summer break. In contrast, Green's regional mathematics conference occurred only once yearly over a three-day weekend. The kind of reading and writing enjoyed by King and Nichols could happen almost anytime, whereas Nichols's critical friends group met only one evening per month. These patterns reveal an attribute of this kind of reflection: its occurrence can be unpredictable. Whereas this flexibility can be an asset, giving teachers the freedom to reflect how and when they want and for reasons that seem best to them, it can also be a drawback, for reflection can just as easily *not* take place. The incredible worth the teachers attributed to their reflective activities in personal contexts makes this situation troubling. It seems somewhat disconcerting that the experiences that touched the teachers in deep and meaningful ways were primarily left to chance.

The Challenges and Benefits of Reflecting in Personal Contexts

Throughout the cases of teachers' personally selected activities, their passion for reflection was evident. Here, we review the benefits that made these experiences so valuable in the eyes of the teachers, which primarily involved the integration of the intellectual examination of teaching with the affective warmth and comfort of collegiality. We also examine what could be a challenge for reflection in these contexts: the potential exclusion of other teachers from the opportunities.

The integration of intellect and affect. The benefits of reflecting in the personal contexts included learning about teaching, getting new ideas, strengthening collegial relationships, integrating personal and professional lives, and helping teachers feel inspired in their work. These were true for reflective as well as nonreflective experiences, calling attention to features of activities that the teachers felt were valuable on many levels.

The paradox of voluntary participation. The glowing reports of these teachers as they looked back on their reflective experiences showed a negative side: few teachers participated in the activities. At issue in these self-selected activities was their apparent failure to reach many teachers. A group of ten, a group of four, a group of two, a single one—these were the numbers of teachers involved in the opportunities.

Of course, any of these opportunities could potentially be arranged to involve far more teachers in a number of ways. Indeed, some were publicly offered through the school; many simply required teacher choice to participate. But according to the teachers' reports, such opportunities weren't always inclusive. Lack of time, funding, interest, and awareness prohibited teachers from opting into the activities in large numbers. The teachers who did participate sought out the opportunities or created them themselves. In a sense, the experiences described in this section seemed to succeed *because* of their distance from an educational structure that left little chance for such interaction and from the sometimes constraining foci of particular programs. Thus, a challenge of reflecting in personal contexts was overcoming the paradox that smaller groups seemed to be powerful forums for reflection, but that smaller groups also reached fewer teachers at a time.

An essential point of this section is that teachers highly valued the benefits of reflective experiences that honored the professional and personal sides of teaching. However, making such experiences accessible to all teachers requires attention, time, possibly money, and probably training— as well as an acceptance that reflection in any number of forms is a valuable element of teachers' work.

LESSONS LEARNED ABOUT TEACHERS
REFLECTING ON THEIR OWN

The difference between the personal contexts and the other contexts is astonishing and has implications for what matters for teachers in reflecting on practice. Compared with teachers' experiences in schools and programs for teacher assessment, the reflection that surfaced when teachers came together in personally selected contexts was rewarding, engaging, helpful, meaningful, and suited to each teacher. Activities were virtually teeming with reflective opportunities. Talking together for hours, the teachers could delve deeply into issues that concerned them and see the conversation through to its natural, usually beneficial conclusion. Other activities were less reflective but contributed to teachers' enrichment in other ways. None of the activities in this context worked directly against reflection, as they sometimes did in the other contexts. The discussion below highlights themes across the cases for an overview of the effectiveness of reflection in personal contexts.

The Ability to Foster Reflection

As much as the teachers enjoyed the experiences highlighted in this section, the activities were less consistently effective in supporting reflection than those in the other two contexts. Nonreflective time was a feature of every case.

However, the elements that *did* foster reflection were also described by the teachers as being more highly valued than activities in any other context. The teachers who were involved in collegial communities were effusive in their praise of the activities and the people involved; at times, they could barely find the words to express their gratitude for these opportunities. The teachers felt connected with their colleagues, motivated by the conversation, inspired by the relationships, and absorbed by the content in a way that made their other experiences with reflection seem practically barren.

A Foundation of Trust

Unlike in the other two contexts, a great many of the teachers' experiences in the personal context were valuable *despite* being nonreflective. These included spending time with the colleagues whose company they enjoyed, being inspired and renewed as a result of group meetings or conferences, participating in professional organizations, and engaging in conversations about content-related topics. It may seem surprising to focus on such events in a book on reflection, but because the teachers valued them so highly, they offer insight into how activities might be structured for teachers more generally—insight that can be used to support reflective practice. Nonreflective aspects of activities created a foundation of trust from which reflection became possible.

The Consistency of Significance

One final distinction made experiences in the personal context notable: this context was the only one in which *every* reflective experience struck the teachers as significant to their learning and the learning of their students. And yet the opportunity for teachers to create such activities in the actual context of their work was largely absent—a finding that was clear in the contexts of schools and programs, as well. Those who would foster reflection for teachers must absolutely address this contradiction and make room and resources for teachers to design the kinds of reflective activities that they believe contribute so highly to their practice.

These findings about the teachers' experiences in the personal context suggest that such experiences have much to offer in terms of ways to structure reflection for teachers, including another set of advantages and disadvantages. These are discussed below.

Advantages of Reflecting on One's Own

Given the enthusiasm the teachers had for the experiences in this context, one can imagine that they held numerous advantages. These advantages fall into three categories: community, culture, and a respect for the whole teacher.

Community. The most obvious aspect of the personal context was the strength of the community involved. The teachers liked, respected, and trusted each other. They were friends as much as they were colleagues, and they reflected collaboratively in ways that simply didn't occur in other contexts. Nichols's critical friends group exemplified this sense of community—one that seemed transformative when compared with collegial groups in other settings, such as the department meetings and even her own lunchtime study group.

Culture. This was the only context in which culture was an asset. None of the activities in the personal context suffered from the constraints of the school structure and culture or the demands of assessment programs; rather, they were purposefully separated from those contexts and thus existed in protected time and space. Perhaps because the home environment, conference settings, and other locations held more personal connotations for teachers than did their schools, the benefits were memorable. The teachers felt cared for, trusted, trusting, safe to expose their weaknesses, and free to share honest opinions, questions, and fears—feelings possible only in a culture of safety and trust.

Respect for the whole teacher. The personal side of teachers' lives was very much a part of reflection in this context, as seen in the thrill of Green's winning a door prize, the support demonstrated at the critical friend's group, and the changes associated with Underwood's upcoming wedding. In the activities that the teachers designed for themselves, there was no separation of the person and the professional as was so evident, for example, in programs of teacher assessment. Emotions and anecdotes were invited in a way rarely glimpsed in the school context. As a result, in these contexts, the teachers seemed more comfortable and more genuine in their interactions *and* their reflection.

Disadvantages of Reflecting on One's Own

If the advantages of experiences in this context could be consistently coupled with powerful learning experiences, they might be ideal models for reflective activities. But the experiences described in this section also had a down side. Disadvantages were related to quality of reflection and time for reflection.

Quality of reflection. The term "quality" here refers to an external perspective on the teachers' reflection, as opposed to the teachers' own perceived value; it refers to a contradiction: even though the teachers believed their activities in this context led to improved learning, when compared with activities in other contexts there was less evidence that this was so.

On one hand, the teachers highly valued the activities. Whether they involved talking, thinking, reading, or writing, the teachers believed the activities helped them improve students' learning and increase their chances for success. By choosing their own reflective activities in accordance with their own needs, goals, interests, and personal styles, the teachers felt they were able to meet their goals of becoming better teachers.

However, as much as the teachers enjoyed the activities, it was also true that their experiences seemed less significant than those in other contexts in terms of professional learning and growth. With two vivid exceptions— Greta's experience as the focus teacher in the critical friends group and Green's growth as a mathematics teacher through conferences—the teachers weren't consistently learning about teaching in a way that directly impacted student learning. In this respect, programs such as the National Board and one-to-one mentoring seemed to be more productive in moving teachers from reflection to implementation, action, and changes in practice. In this context, the teachers sometimes lacked the capacity or the inclination to take on the hardest issues, and sometimes simply let them go in favor of more manageable or more pleasant topics.

Time for reflection. Importantly, the activities in this context were much more relaxed than those in others. However, that advantage was somewhat tenuous. The time was protected by the teachers, not the school system. While this wasn't much of a problem in the cases cited here, it could pose a problem for extending such opportunities to other teachers. It was in this regard that the uniqueness of these four teachers most likely affected their experiences, for teachers with their unusual levels of accomplishment, motivation, leadership skills, and expertise are the very sort of people who engage in such activities out of a personal love of learning. One wonders if the opportunities these teachers made for themselves would be found in a similar study of less intrinsically motivated teachers.

The advantages and disadvantages of activities in the personal context shed light on what made successful experiences for teachers in general and for reflection in particular. The wisdom of the teachers themselves was evident in the activities they designed and structured for themselves when they believed that to do so would be well worth the effort.

SUMMARY

The cases of the personal context were identified as such for several reasons. First, they existed outside the normal range of teachers' professional activities; second, they took place on teachers' own time for reasons of personal *and* professional interest; third, they were voluntary activities chosen by teachers for reasons of personal interest, motivation, and zeal. Whether by chance or design, the activities in this context were reflective and valuable in at least one if not several ways.

However, the reflection that surfaced here contrasted with the highly structured and heavily intellectual kinds of reflection in other contexts. Matters for reflection in the personal context were characteristically matters of the heart. Teachers shared quandaries and searched for solutions, followed their passions to inform practice, and used their love of reading, writing, friends, and even sports to help them think through what they were doing and why in their personal and professional lives. These experiences gave the teachers the opportunity to reflect about their teaching and their lives in fundamentally integrated ways.

The past several sections have explored the multiple, if sometimes overwhelming, matters for reflection in school contexts, the intellectual aspect of reflection in programs of teacher assessment, and the sense of fulfillment teachers experienced in reflection on their own. The next chapter pays special attention to those activities perceived as most valuable by the teachers in a discussion of the results of the study. We now move to the final section of the book, which summarizes what we can learn from all three of the contexts—professional, programmatic, and personal—and discusses what really matters in supporting teachers' reflection.

Chapter Twenty-One

Lessons Learned Across Contexts

What really matters in teachers' reflection? In this book, we have explored teachers' experiences with reflection to discover more about the nature of reflection in teaching, the conditions that foster reflection, and teachers' perceptions of their experiences with reflection. Although the cases presented in the previous chapters are only samples of all of the instances of reflection found and analyzed for the research, they nevertheless reveal a varied set of experiences in each of three overarching contexts: (1) the professional (or school-based) context of teachers' everyday lives, including meetings, conversations, and time spent in the classrooms; (2) programmatic (or program-centered) contexts such as the certification process for the National Board for Professional Teaching Standards, other voluntary programs for teacher assessment, and mentoring programs; and (3) personal contexts highlighting teachers' activities on their own time, specifically a critical friends group, a regional conference, and activities such as reading, writing, and thinking. These experiences ranged from powerful to trivial. What can we learn about reflection from the diversity of the teachers' experiences? What characteristics were shared by those experiences the teachers identified as most valuable? These two questions frame the discussion in this chapter, which presents lessons learned by examining the cases.

To review, a single, comprehensive definition of reflection was used to identify the reflective experiences of the four teachers:

Looking back on experience in a way that informs practice, learning in the midst of practice, and/or making informed and intelligent decisions about what to do, when to do it, and why it should be done. (Shulman, 1987; Richert, 1990; Schön, 1983)

178

Drawn from the literature on reflection, this definition resounded with the teachers, who unanimously agreed with it—in Green's case, exclaiming, "Yes! That makes perfect sense!" Despite this apparent congruence between the definition, the research on reflection, and four accomplished teachers' opinions, reflection was manifested in different ways for each of the teachers and in each of the contexts.

When we look across their experiences, three salient themes become clear regarding the nature of teachers' reflection:

1. Contextual factors directly and indirectly affect the occurrence of reflection.
2. The quality and value of reflection depend upon the nature of related activities.
3. Boosts and barriers to reflection derive from teachers' unique intentions, the conditions of any experience, and challenges inherent in any given situation.

These three themes of the research are discussed at greater length below.

CONTEXTS AFFECTING REFLECTION

The cases of teachers' experiences were arranged by three overarching contexts that comprised their professional lives: the professional, programmatic, and personal contexts. The cases revealed that *contexts differ in their ability to foster reflection.*

The Professional Context

In the professional context, competing agendas and the structures of schools constrained the teachers' opportunities to reflect on their practice. Of particular note was the division between potentially reflective opportunities structured by administrators and those initiated by the teachers themselves.

Overall, the teachers' unanimous insistence that occurrences of reflection were rare to nonexistent in their day-to-day jobs created a persuasive argument that *the professional context more often prevented or remained neutral about reflection than it encouraged opportunities to reflect on practice.* This was evidenced by the lack of apparent reflection in staff and department meetings and by the severe time constraints on teachers' opportunities to address the multiple matters for reflection that arose. However, subtleties were apparent between administrator-led and teacher-initiated activities.

Administrator-led activities typically precluded or failed to support reflection. Reflective opportunities in this context were rare. Only a few administrator-led activities managed to structure reflection for teachers. Examples included King's administrators' attempts to engage teachers in setting department goals and Underwood's faculty discussion about ways to personalize the school. The teachers more often than not found little of value for themselves in these activities and they didn't always take them seriously.

In contrast to the typical absence or ineffectiveness of opportunities for reflection structured by administrators, *teacher-initiated opportunities either sought or supported reflection.* These included the teachers' reflection behind the scenes, during, after, and between classes. Surprisingly, the same teachers who sometimes seemed harried, disgruntled, or apathetic as they sat in required meetings turned out to have rich reflective lives in the privacy of their classrooms and their conversations. Granted, the teachers didn't always have the time, perspective, or capacity to reflect on the issues they faced, but when they did reflect, they were quite adept at structuring reflection for themselves.

Interestingly, the two categories of reflective opportunities in this context—administrator-led and teacher-initiated—were distinguished in part by the freedom the teachers had to guide their own reflection. As a result, administrator-led activities often constrained reflection and teacher-led opportunities often supported it. These two halves of experience were combined in the programmatic context.

The Programmatic Context

Compared with the professional context, reflection was much more evident in the programmatic context. Opportunities to reflect were designed to be part of programs such as the National Board and voluntary programs of teacher assessment. However, each of those opportunities was seen to have both reflective and nonreflective counterparts. *In this context, program design specifically targeted reflection as a goal, but required additional effort not related to the goal of reflection.*

Because reflection was specifically designed into the programs, reflective opportunities were abundant in this context. Programs structured and supported such activities in an impressive number of ways. Materials such as books, software, guidelines, and questions all evidenced intentional efforts to invite and nurture teachers' reflection.

Unfortunately, *reflective opportunities were accompanied by less productive, nonreflective counterparts.* In some cases, the very process designed to aid reflection became a burden that impinged on teachers' ability to reflect. For instance, in King's pilot teacher-assessment program, more time was spent organizing the project than in conducting the activities designed to guide reflection. In contrast, mentoring programs minimized the need for administrative activities; thus reflection was realized with relative ease.

Overall, the programs involved the same tension between freedom and structure seen in the school context. The difference was that, in the professional context, teachers experienced both reflective and nonreflective activities, whereas in the programmatic context reflective and nonreflective components coexisted within each single activity.

The Personal Context

Of the three contexts, the personal context was the most welcoming of reflection. Tensions between the teachers' needs and the requirements of others (e.g., administrators or programs) did not exist in this context, in which even the nonreflective counterparts of activities seemed to benefit the teachers in some way. Thus, *in the personal context, opportunities consistently encouraged reflection.*

Opportunities to reflect positively abounded in this context. Some activities, such as the critical friends protocol, were quite structured and guided teachers in their reflection. Others, such as Nichols's writing, were unstructured and freed teachers to reflect as they wished, about whatever they wanted. Reflection didn't require the sometimes overwhelming components found in activities in other contexts. Rather, the *teachers' self-selected, self-initiated contexts either structured and supported reflection or at least provided the opportunity to reflect on practice*—and either approach could be effective.

As in the other two contexts, reflective opportunities were accompanied by nonreflective counterparts; but in this context, *the nonreflective aspects held value.* What was truly astounding in the personal context was the joy with which the teachers engaged in these aspects of the activities. Whether they lingered over dinner with colleagues, participated in conference-session entertainment, or contemplated life issues in solitude, the teachers reported that they purposely chose to participate on their own time. They frequently related stories of these experiences with delight and expressions of gratitude.

The trends described above highlight the most striking differences between the contexts, reinforcing the assertion that context has bearing on whether and how reflection takes place. In this study, no single context emerged as being perfect for reflection; each of the three contexts provided some opportunity for reflection and each limited reflection to some degree or in some manner. But the teachers' opinions of the activities available to them ranged significantly, leading to the next point, which focuses not just on whether and when reflection took place, but also on which activities the teachers found meaningful.

THE QUALITY AND VALUE OF REFLECTION

Another theme across all of the cases was that simply *designing an activity to be reflective does not ensure either that it will indeed be reflective in practice (i.e., that it will be effective) or that it will be considered valuable by teachers.* This point differentiates between two significant perspectives: (1) the researcher's (an outside perspective), which is concerned with the quality and depth of the reflection, as well as the effectiveness of an activity in prompting it, and (2) the teachers' (an inside perspective), which provides insight regarding teachers' sense of satisfaction or value. Considering both the effectiveness and value of activities is important when structuring reflective opportunities for teachers.

The Effectiveness of Activities for Structuring Reflection

The research for this book involved analyzing each case. Was the activity effective in helping teachers to reflect? If so, how effective was it in fostering reflection in some depth or quality? Asking this revealed that the relative *effectiveness of activities for structuring reflection varied in different activities.* Some activities were *substantive;* others were more *superficial.* Very little research is available on effectiveness (but see, e.g., Collier, 1999), but the data for this study highlighted its importance. Consider three examples.

In an example from the professional context, Nichols's lunchtime study group discussed strategies for reflecting on practice. In this example, the teachers' reflection was largely descriptive. They identified a matter for reflection and considered it, *without* moving very far in their own thinking or reporting any changes in practice that might improve teaching or learning. This example is representative of the finding that the *least effective activities were associated with descriptive, somewhat superficial reflection.*

In another example from the same context, Underwood explained how a nagging feeling about his chemistry class—that it had too much reading at the beginning and too many labs at the end—informed his thinking and his teaching. He compared his feeling with his colleagues' perceptions of the same class and used the information to restructure it. By incorporating alternative perspectives and using concrete evidence from practice, he was able to see his practice from another angle. As a result, his reflection was more substantial and analytical than that in the example above. This case illustrates that *moderately effective activities were associated with alternative perspectives and analytical reflection.*

In a third example, Green described an inspired moment in her practice that she directly related to reflection. She discovered that merely placing a piece of scrap paper on algebra students' desks helped them get straight to work on their assignments. These students, Green reported, were students with a history of failing marks in mathematics. Rather than give up on them, as she worried others had done, she found a way to reach them and help them learn a subject they found difficult. Even this brief review of the example suggests that she took on some critical questions. What was it about these particular students that made them struggle so with math? How were they being ill served and what could she do to improve their learning? These were the kinds of questions underlying her actions—questions not addressed in either of the two other examples above. This example incorporated the analysis of student work and the description of the situation evident in the two previous examples, but Green went farther with her reflection, resulting in action on her part and that of her students. The reflection was more than just a descriptive puzzle of practice and more than an analytical response to students' work. It was a substantial and meaningful experience that she believed helped her change an unsatisfactory situation into one in which her students could learn. This example is representative of the finding that the *most effective activities were associated with critical questions and initiated changes in classroom practice.*

The three examples above represent cases of reflection at different levels of quality or depth. As we can see, what counts as "reflection" can range from a somewhat superficial description of practice, to analysis that incorporates alternative perspectives, to a kind of critical questioning that asks which students are not being served and how they can be helped to learn. To date, no clear language exists in the literature to distinguish carefully between these levels of quality. Instead, all kinds of experiences go by the name of reflection with no way to know how to name, much less prompt or support, the most significant kinds of reflection. Thus, one area in which more research is needed involves comparing activities according to how effective they are in structuring reflection in general and, specifically, in achieving reflection of more quality or depth. Those who structure reflective activities for teachers should be aware of the importance of moving teachers along the continuum from superficial to substantive reflection.

Teachers' Perceived Value of Experiences

Another measure of the teachers' experiences in the research for this book included an analysis of the teachers' thoughts about their own experiences with reflection. This revealed that the *teachers' perceived value of experiences also varied in different activities.* What differentiated the most valuable experiences from the least valuable? This is important to discuss in a book intended to inform efforts to structure reflective activities for teachers.

The group of instances that the teachers found the least meaningful included those designed or required by administrators and programs—many of which were not effective in structuring reflection. *Consistently, the least valuable instances were distinctly removed from classroom issues.*

Rather, they focused on issues such as state standards, school goals, and disciplinary matters *without* tying those directly to the teachers' interactions with students in their classes.

In contrast, moderately valuable activities were closely related to teachers' classroom practice. Instances included habitual, everyday reflection on practice at the end of the day, including reflection as a part of programs of teacher assessment. As a group, *moderately valuable activities helped teachers clarify what they were doing and why, without necessarily prompting changes in existing practice.*

Almost every example of the experiences that the teachers found most meaningful incorporated the needs, thoughts, ideas, and progress of students, whether through direct conversation, classroom interaction, or written work. In every single instance of reflection that the teachers found most meaningful, the relationship between teaching and learning was of the essence. The teachers either recognized a problem of student learning and changed their practice to solve it or they improved their teaching and marveled at the impact on students. Across all contexts, the *most meaningful activities often involved student input; benefits were clearly related to improved teaching and learning.*

Above, we have just uncovered an important distinction between the *effectiveness* of reflective activities and the *value* of activities as perceived by the teachers. Whereas effectiveness relates to the power of an activity to motivate teachers' deep reflective thinking about practice, value relates to teachers' beliefs about an activity, such as how much they enjoyed it and how much they benefited from it (both personally and professionally). The distinction between the effectiveness and value of activities is an important one to consider with respect to structuring reflective opportunities for teachers, for both have implications for what such opportunities should ideally be. A summary of the activities in the cases illustrates the distinction between effectiveness (e.g., reflective or nonreflective) and perceived value (valuable or not valuable) in table 21.1.

That these categories existed makes two important statements about teacher learning with respect to reflection. First, that an opportunity was designed to be reflective does not guarantee its effectiveness in fostering reflection. Second, that an activity is reflective does not mean it will be valuable to teachers. Let us discuss this in more detail.

Table 21.1.   Quality of Reflection in Cases of Reflection

	Not Valuable	*Valuable*
Nonreflective	• Some staff meetings (including typical and special-project) • Some department meetings • Some collegial conversations • Administrative system of teacher evaluation • Some activities between classes and after school (e.g., administrative tasks of teaching and validation of questionable practice) • Technical aspects of portfolio creation (creation of videotapes, choosing student work to analyze, some writing) Some conversations with colleagues	• Some conversations with colleagues • Some activities between classes and after school (e.g., some planning and grading) • Administrative tasks and organization of activities for voluntary assessment programs • Social/business aspects of critical friends meetings • Social aspects of conferences • Social chatting
Reflective	• Some special project staff meetings • Some conversations with colleagues • Some instances of reflecting on standards and guidelines (e.g., when teachers' practice meets standards)	• Some special-project staff meetings • Some department meetings • Some collegial conversations • Professional growth systems of teacher evaluation • Students' evaluations of teachers • Reflection (in midst of instruction) • Some activities between classes and after school (e.g., looking back and assessing the day) • Reflecting on standards • Examination of videotaped teaching • Analyzing student work • Reflective aspects of voluntary assessment programs • Joint reflection with student teacher/cooperating teacher • Some peer-helper relationships • Critical friends groups • Conference sessions • Reading, chatting, journaling (when linked to practice) • Solitary thought

Reflection to Support Quality Teaching

There were some cases in which the teachers found activities to be very valuable experiences, often because they prompted reflection. Importantly, almost every example was voluntarily undertaken by the teachers. For example, the most valuable experiences in the professional context were those initiated by teachers to solve pressing problems. The most valuable experiences in the programmatic contexts included those that gave teachers new ideas or helped them dramatically improve practice. The most valuable experiences in the personal contexts were those in which teachers learned something substantial that had the potential to impact student learning. Consistently, the teachers went to great lengths to make these experiences successful, expending extra effort, personal time, and even their own money to reflect on their practice in ways that they believed helped their students learn. Therefore, *teachers' experiences that were both reflective and valuable seemed to support quality teaching.*

Lost Opportunities for Reflection

Cases that the teachers perceived as nonreflective and not valuable consisted largely of meetings or activities in which they were obligated to participate—such as staff meetings, department meetings, and traditional forms of teacher evaluation. Most of these activities were not designed to be reflective—although the teachers' reactions to these experiences suggested that some room for reflection might have been a welcome change. This was especially true in cases in which reflection wasn't invited, but the teachers nevertheless raised critical issues—for example that the curriculum didn't suit the needs of their students, that resources were being wasted, or that students were reacting apathetically to their lessons. This suggested that the activities in this category could, and possibly should, be organized for reflection around the issues that arose but remained unaddressed. Thus, *teachers' experiences that were neither reflective nor valuable were lost opportunities.*

Reflection as Going Through the Motions

Some activities were reflective, but not valuable, as when teachers went through the motions of reflection without discovering new meaning.

Activities supposedly designed to invite reflection periodically failed to do so, resulting in less-than-inspiring exercises in task completion. A number of these occurred in the professional context. Examples included meetings in which teachers were asked to prove how they were meeting school and state goals. Other examples included paradoxical cases in which teachers' reflection validated questionable practice, as when they said a lesson had gone well, even though students hadn't understood the concepts. These were reflective by definition, but superficial nevertheless.

Examples such as these warrant attention, because they provide information about what works and what doesn't in attempting to structure reflective opportunities for teachers. *The teachers' experiences that were reflective, but not valuable, revealed discrepancies between the intent and the outcome of supposedly "reflective" activities.*

The lighter side of reflection. Some of the most valuable experiences, from the teachers' perspective, were found to be nonreflective. Concentrated in the personal context, teachers often engaged in playful, interesting, and light-hearted activities that were important to them. Casual banter at Nichols's critical friends group was one example; Green's joy at winning a door prize at the mathematics conference was another. Although these experiences perhaps seem off topic in a book about teachers' reflection, the reported value they held for teachers made them significant. *The teachers' experiences that were not reflective, but valuable, offered important clues about what motivated teachers to take part in activities, with implications for encouraging reflection.*

The above categories of reflective experiences illustrate a significant finding about what happens when teachers' perceptions are honored as part of the research process. The teachers in this study—accomplished teachers recognized for their leadership and expertise—revealed that the activities arranged by other people (such as administrators and program developers) have a tendency to miss the mark. As a result, these teachers often took responsibility for their own reflection and their own learning.

BARRIERS AND BOOSTS TO REFLECTION

Whereas previous themes focused on the impact on reflection of the different contexts of teachers' professional lives, this theme focuses on the roles of individuals and their unique situations. Three conclusions can be drawn from this perspective: first, the intentionality of individual teachers had bearing on the success of an activity and the resulting reflection; second, certain conditions supported and encouraged reflection; and third, barriers existed that threatened even the best intentions and conditions. *Regardless of context or activity, reflection depends upon these features to be successful.*

Teachers' Intentionality

The term "*intentionality*" is used to highlight a teacher's intention to reflect on a given matter at a given time. This was a significant factor, for almost regardless of context or activity, *the teachers' motivation and self-initiation determined whether or not reflection took place.* Where opportunities for reflection were lacking, the teachers tried to create them; when opportunities for reflection seemed meaningless, they avoided them as best they could. They opted into or out of the activities.

Intentionality was important to the emergence of reflection, given the scarcity of structured opportunities to reflect in the teachers' lives. *In the absence of external support from administrators or programs, teachers created their own opportunities for reflection.* They *raised issues, proposed ideas, and set up activities for reflection for themselves and sometimes their colleagues in the course of daily work.* This occurred most frequently in the professional context. Examples included King speaking up in her department meeting to urge other teachers to be reflective regarding student note-taking skills, Nichols arranging a lunchtime study group, and Green initiating conversations about teaching practices as former department chair. These examples say a great deal about the resourcefulness of the teachers in this study, although they don't say much about the available opportunities to reflect in their schools. If these teachers hadn't initiated opportunities for reflection, the opportunities wouldn't have existed.

Intentionality was also important to the success of reflection in the opportunities that did exist. *When support from administrators or programs was available, teachers voluntarily chose whether or not to participate in reflection.* This occurred most frequently in the activities that made up the programmatic and personal contexts. Every one of these experiences was voluntary. Even the mentoring programs, which could be seen as mandatory in the sense that student teaching is required for certification, were voluntary with respect to reflection. After all, both Nichols and Green provided examples of teachers who didn't take the reflective component of the mentoring seriously and managed to complete programs without it. Reasons for participating in the programs varied—such as the status that accompanied National Board certification and the collegiality that was part of the critical friends group. Regardless of their reasons for participating, the teachers voluntarily sought and became committed to activities that required reflection—sometimes extensive and challenging reflection, at that.

Analysis of the activities in which teachers' commitment to reflection was present, compared with those in which it was not, revealed that their intentionality was not whimsical or unpredictable. Rather, the *teachers' intentionality was related to the goals and benefits of an activity.* Patterns in the cases revealed that when the goals of reflection were *not* clearly related to teaching and learning, the benefits were seen as negligible and teachers' interest was slight. However, when the goals of reflection were potentially, presumably, or intentionally related to teaching and learning, teachers' interest was piqued; they engaged in reflection. Those instances when that potential was realized ignited the passion of teachers and drove them to make what they described as noteworthy changes in practice that significantly impacted students' lives.

This finding was so strong that *perceived benefits to student learning actually seemed to determine whether or not reflection took place.* Seeing no direct benefit toward this end, the teachers opted out of reflection. This was evident when reflective activities were carefully crafted to prompt teachers' reflection for some other purpose, such as aligning curriculum with state standards. The only exception was when teachers saw some other benefit, as was the case with many of the teachers' National Board experiences. At these times, even when the teachers perceived the benefits for their own and students' learning to be minimal or only moderate, they nevertheless jumped through the various hoops of the activities for the sake of certification.

Thus, the teachers' intentionality influenced whether or not reflection took place. However, intention alone was not sufficient to ensure the most effective or valuable kind of experience, for even their best efforts were vulnerable to conditions and barriers that sometimes hindered reflection. Fostering reflection involved not only caring about the potential influence on teaching and learning, but also putting into place the necessary conditions and removing the barriers that prevented the actualization of reflection.

Conditions Supporting Reflection

In addition to intentionality, the success of activities depended on conditions supporting, encouraging, and protecting reflection. The two were actually related: *conditions supporting reflection determined whether or not reflection took place, provided teachers' intentionality was also present.* The different scenarios this relationship created will be elaborated below, but first it seems important to discuss briefly what the conditions were that supported reflection.

To conclusively identify the many elements that influence conditions for reflection would require more extensive data than are available in this research. However, several conditions were frequently present in the activities that were identified as effective in structuring reflection for the teachers. *Conditions included a climate in which reflection was valued, teachers' capacity for reflection, materials to guide the activity, and time to reflect.* No single one of these conditions seemed to be a prerequisite, but together they were found to support reflection.

As noted above, the presence of these conditions did not ensure that reflection would take place. *Conditions conducive to reflection did not support reflection if teachers' intentionality was absent (i.e., the benefits were not evidently intended to improve teaching and learning).* One example of this was King's department meeting, in which teachers were required to reflect on the department's goals and their relationship to the school's priorities. By designing the activity, administrators indicated they valued the teachers' input; charts and questions were available to guide the reflection; and several hours during a teacher workday were devoted to the task. Nevertheless, as King explained, the activity had an air of inauthenticity. Seeing no benefit for themselves or their students, the teachers filled out the chart without reflecting on the issues as administrators had hoped. The benefits were not evidently intended to improve teaching and learning, so the fact that the conditions were conducive to reflection didn't seem to make a difference. The teachers devalued the activity.

Even though conditions alone did not ensure the occurrence of reflection, they did seem to play a critical role in the success of reflective opportunities. *Conditions* not *conducive to reflection minimized the value of reflection, even if teachers' intentionality was present (i.e., the benefits were intended to improve teaching and learning).* One example of this was found in Nichols's lunchtime study group. In an observed meeting, the teachers seemed to want to reflect on their practice together, so intentionality was present. However, they lacked either the capacity or skills or materials or time to create a substantially reflective activity. Thus, conditions were not conducive to reflection, which minimized the effectiveness of their efforts.

Even though neither conditions nor teachers' intentionality alone was always sufficient to generate reflection, the combination of these two features was powerful. *Conditions conducive to reflection combined with teachers' intentionality resulted in prolific and even profound instances of teacher reflection, including an ability to think deeply, solve problems, improve teaching, and attend to student learning.* Examples included Underwood's inspiration to revamp a lesson as a result of a National Board entry and Green's memorable learning from the mathematics conference. The impressive results when teachers were motivated *and* supported in their efforts emphasized the importance of activities that inspire reflection as well as the conditions that foster it.

However, any discussion of conducive conditions must be informed by an understanding of situations that render attempts at reflection futile: the barriers confronting reflection.

Barriers Confronting Reflection

Perhaps the most disturbing, if not the most surprising, finding of this study was the power of barriers to divert reflection. *Barriers confronting reflection determined whether or not reflection took place, regardless of teachers' intentions or otherwise conducive conditions.* No matter how valuable activities might be, they were constantly faced with barriers limiting their benefits.

Such barriers are numerous, diverse, and complex. They are also too significant to dismiss, so they will be discussed in broad terms below. Primarily, in this study, the *barriers included a climate in which reflection was devalued or criticized, lack of capacity and materials to guide reflection, time, and common features of the work of teaching.* The first three types of barriers seem to be manageable. The designers of reflective activities, whether they are teachers, administrators, or program designers, can easily adopt an ethic that values reflection, help teachers gain the capacity for reflection by teaching them skills or providing materials, and set aside time for that purpose. But the last type of barrier poses an inimitable threat to these efforts, for such barriers are deeply embedded in the current structures of schooling.

As discovered in the research, the teachers' *professional environments were replete with barriers that not only limited, but actually prohibited efforts to sustain reflective practice.* Teachers' participation in programs heaped more challenges on top of those they faced during the school day. Even in the personal contexts, they encountered some kind of challenge. Almost every single case included some obstacle related to culture, capacity, structure, or time. Literature on school reform is teeming with discussion of these barriers (e.g., Sarason, 1990, 1996; Fullan, 1991; Fullan & Miles, 1992), but the four teachers' schools appeared practically untouched by efforts to alleviate the challenges. As witnessed throughout this book, *the profession of teaching was unsupportive of reflection.* This is not to say that the teachers didn't manage to reflect on their practice; they most certainly did. But their strong words about the scarcity of opportunities for reflection, their assertions that reflection often fell last in long lists of priorities, and the consistent tendency for their reflection to occur after hours all painted a picture of teachers reflecting in spite of, not because of, school structures and culture. The tragedy of this reality was that *reflection was considered a luxury, not a necessity*—an attitudinal barrier that had direct bearing on the quality of teaching.

What complicates this point is that many of those barriers seem understandable, considering the situations of teaching; however, they are also unconscionable, considering the needs of teachers and students. For example, Underwood was observed overlooking contradictions between his teaching (which he thought went well) and students' learning (which he acknowledged had not). That he didn't have an alternative perspective with which to compare their perceptions of the lessons seemed reasonable given the isolating nature of teaching (Palmer, 1998); however, that lessons could be considered successful in the absence of student learning seemed unjustifiable. Unfortunately, these were not exceptional instances. They represented the norms of large classes, overcrowded schools, and a host of multiple, sometimes competing responsibilities that made it impossible for teachers to address undesirable events that occurred. Understandable? Perhaps. Acceptable? No. Such matters for reflection positively saturated the school environment, but the many barriers to reflection kept them from tackling even a handful a day.

The point cannot be made strongly enough: *quality teaching and learning depend on the removal of barriers that block teachers' ability to reflect on their practice.* Without the capacity to consider what they are doing and why, without the time and opportunity to learn from their experiences, and without the motivation to let such learning inform their teaching, teachers are likely to let ineffective practices slip by unnoticed. Barriers of school structure and culture consistently threatened the teachers' efforts in each of these areas—a significant problem, considering what was at stake. When they approached their practice reflectively, the teachers were seen to be thoughtful, compassionate, and infinitely capable of helping young people succeed. When they did not, even these well-intentioned, masterful teachers overlooked contradictions, assumptions, and behaviors that were ineffectual, biased, and even harmful. These are strong words that are not used lightly. What is at stake is not just the difference between good and better instructional practice. What is at stake is the well-being of every student and educator in the system. In this light, the elimination of barriers to reflection is crucial, the perpetuation of non-reflective behaviors inexcusable.

SUMMARY

This chapter has reviewed the cases of reflection presented throughout the book and found that they fell into categories of varying degrees of effectiveness and value for teachers—often depending upon contextual factors that either boosted or built barriers to reflection. The next chapter explicitly examines the most valuable cases to learn more about how to structure such experiences for teachers.

Chapter Twenty-Two

The Heart of Quality Teaching

What makes reflection the heart of quality teaching? Reflection motivates continual improvement—a form of inspired professional growth for ever-better teaching and learning. This chapter explores the centrality of reflection in quality teaching, especially because of its relationship to professional growth. It presents practical implications about reflection drawn from the cases, with a focus on the most valuable experiences. The book concludes with a call for emphasizing reflection as an element of quality teaching and asserts the need for explicit recognition in schools, in programs, and by teachers of the significance of reflection in teaching and learning.

PRACTICAL IMPLICATIONS: BEYOND REFLECTION TO PROFESSIONAL GROWTH

All of the activities the teachers perceived as being very valuable were also reflective by the definition used in this study, supporting the widely held belief that reflection is an important component of teacher learning (Ball & Cohen, 1999; Darling-Hammond & Sykes, 1999; Hawley & Valli, 1999). We call these valuable experiences "professional growth experiences"—valuable experiences that incorporated reflection in the service of teacher learning.

"Professional growth experiences" in this chapter are defined as experiences that teachers found intrinsically meaningful—not just because they enjoyed them, but also because they provided an opportunity to reflect and to learn something new that had the potential to improve teaching and learning. This way of thinking about a teacher's professional growth incorporates the concept of reflection and explicitly names the goal of teacher learning—a goal based on the assumption that teacher quality is closely tied to an ability to continually improve practice.

It should be noted that a goal of the research was not to examine these "professional growth experiences" in depth, for their existence didn't even become apparent until the final stages of analysis. Nevertheless, it is possible to discuss characteristics of the most valuable experiences in broad terms. To reiterate, the professional growth opportunities included those experiences that the teachers perceived as highly valuable, that incorporated reflection, and for which there was evidence that the teachers learned something new, with the potential to improve practice and student learning. The next section discusses shared characteristics of these cases—an important step in designing and encouraging such experiences.

Characteristics of Professional Growth Experiences

The teachers' praise for professional growth experiences sent a strong message that these experiences were perceived as valuable, important, and successful. Five attributes characterized the experiences: a connection to a vision of teaching and learning, the ability to inspire teachers' commitment, the capacity to meet the developmental needs of teachers, a positive and conducive culture, and the use of teacher leadership. In many cases, a sixth attribute affected professional growth: the role of administrators. These attributes of professional growth experiences are discussed in more detail later in this chapter.

Connection to a Vision of Quality Teaching and Learning

The teachers' reflection in these cases was guided by a vision of quality teaching and learning, whether that vision was explicit (as outlined by standards) or implicit (as in implied beliefs underlying comments on teaching). Their reflection was motivated by a comparison of what was with what ought to be and driven by a motivation to more closely align the two. For example, Nichols's colleague (Greta) discovered that students weren't succeeding with writing and asked her critical friends group for help in changing the lesson. In this way, she sought to improve her practice so that it met a higher standard of student learning.

Even though a vision of teaching and learning was present in each of the professional growth experiences, the existence of that vision alone didn't ensure the experience would be valuable. On the contrary, life became frustrating when teachers embodied the vision but had to work harder than necessary to prove it (e.g., Green's experience with her National Board entries); or life became tedious when their practice was already consistent with the vision (e.g., King's experience with the pilot evaluation). Thus, vision is only one of many characteristics that make an experience meaningful for teachers.

Ability to Inspire a Sense of Commitment

In the professional growth experiences, activities succeeded or faltered by virtue of the teachers' commitment.

To illustrate this, consider three of Underwood's cases. Underwood described no less than three identifiable attempts to get him to reflect on his practice with respect to the school goal of improving students' reading abilities. First, administrators required the department to discuss how they were meeting school goals for student learning, of which reading was one. According to Underwood, the activity was superficial and didn't help him learn. Second, Underwood set a goal of improving reading for students for his evaluation. Although Underwood said he was "taking the goal seriously," he didn't seem to have learned from the experience or to have reflected on the goal. Third, Underwood asked students to evaluate his class. This time, he was finally inspired to improve student reading. The students' feedback encouraged him to have them read a book related to their interests and to a major concept in the course; he then planned to incorporate the book into the syllabus. In this way, Underwood managed to meet the school goal of emphasizing reading, to engage students in science in a way that they found meaningful, to advance his purpose of teaching concepts of microbiology, and, eventually, to improve his practice. In these three events, Underwood showed three different faces: one openly resistant, a second somewhat indifferent, and the third thoughtful, caring, interested, innovative, and engaged.

This example illustrates a common tendency across the professional growth experiences regarding teachers' ownership. When the teachers cared about an issue, situation, or problem, they attended to it, unless counterproductive barriers and conditions prevented them from doing so. When they didn't care, they dismissed the opportunity. Attempts to coerce, require, or otherwise manipulate teachers to reflect were unsuccessful and were viewed with suspicion and distaste by teachers who in other circumstances were intrinsically motivated and reflective. The recommendation here seems obvious: to encourage teachers to reflect on their practice and give them the freedom and opportunity to reflect on meaningful issues that arise in their work.

Capacity to Meet the Developmental Needs of Teachers

Related to the notion of developmental need is that of appropriateness: reflection must meet the needs of the teacher in the particular circumstance. The term "appropriateness" is borrowed from Applebee and Langer's theory of teaching and learning (Applebee & Langer, 1983; Langer & Applebee, 1986). Although their writing focuses on instructional tasks of reading and writing, their definition of appropriateness applies to learning tasks more generally. They write, "The most appropriate tasks will be those that involve abilities that have not yet matured but are in the process of maturation, or in Vygotsky's terms, abilities that are not so much 'ripe' as 'ripening'" (Langer & Applebee, 1986, p. 170). The term "appropriateness" applied to teachers' professional learning experiences emphasizes the importance of challenging teachers at individually appropriate levels.

The appropriateness of an activity designed to foster reflection may depend on the developmental level of the teacher on a continuum from novice to expert; it may depend on the identity of teachers and their life experiences; it may depend on the experiences of teachers and their extant challenges and needs. Each of these situations surfaced in the research for this book and no pattern was clear. What was clear was that an activity that Underwood found meaningful was simplistic for Nichols; what was useless for Green was productive for King. Exactly what makes a reflective experience also a learning experience is apparently related to its appropriateness for each teacher's unique needs—emphasizing the need for an accepted degree of variability among reflective activities.

Positive and Conducive Culture

The term "culture" can be used to discuss elements of any social situation, including relationships, norms, emotional climate, expectations, and more. Various aspects of culture distinguished the most successful cases from their less-effective counterparts. Most of these were intangible, such as a feeling of mutual respect and trust in teachers as responsible and worthy professionals, unique and sensitive individuals, or qualified and appreciated experts. These and other aspects of culture manifested themselves differently in different situations. A few examples described below fall into three categories: personal connection, intellectual challenge, and puzzles of practice.

In their most highly prized experiences, like Nichols's critical friends group, Kings' restaurant group, Green's mathematics conference, and Underwood's conversations with his colleagues, the teachers experienced *personal connection.* The teachers and their colleagues cared about each other and cared for each other, nurturing the person as well as the professional. They listened, connected, shared honest thoughts in ways that exceeded the apparent expectations of their jobs, and contributed to each other's personal development.

Other experiences, namely the National Board certification process, were less nurturing but provided the opportunity for an *intellectual challenge.* Whether they had ten years of experience, like Underwood, or thirty, like Nichols, every one of the teachers was challenged in one way or another to be an even better teacher than before. The process may have been "brutal," as one teacher described it, but it was also satisfying and rewarding, both during and after. Even when the process was behind them, the teachers continued to receive accolades, honors, opportunities, and benefits from having attained the status of National Board certified teacher, each of which—in a profession known for being thankless— validated their worth.

A third group of the teachers' experiences seemed neither nurturing nor intellectually challenging, but somehow prompted genuine learning that the teachers cherished. These included situations in which the teachers worked through *puzzles of practice,* as when Green spontaneously realized that giving reluctant students special pieces of paper to use in their assignments actually increased their tendency to work. In this and similar situations, the teachers were confronted with classroom experiences that prompted them to do things differently. It is significant that these experiences took place where and when they did—in the teachers' classrooms or at home after school, where they had the freedom to reflect on whatever matter struck their attention, in whatever manner they chose and whenever it felt most useful to do so. This underscores one of the themes presented in the previous chapter. When teachers initiated their own reflective activities, they were also able to create the culture they needed to reflect on their own.

These examples illustrate the importance of culture in professional growth experiences, emphasizing the impact of certain elements (e.g., emotions, attitudes, and atmosphere) on reflection.

Use of Teacher Leadership

In professional growth experiences, the teachers commonly exhibited leadership. This form of leadership rests on the assumption that people change organizations by empowering themselves to initiate the changes they wish to see (Senge, 1990). Some examples of the teachers' leadership were:

Taking the initiative: King took the initiative for her own learning and growth as she "reflected out loud" with her husband over an article for use in class, without any apparent external motivation.

Serving as a role model: Green served as a reflective role model for student teachers, much in the way she reported her cooperating teacher served as a role model for her.

Accepting a challenge: Underwood confronted the challenges of overhauling lessons to meet the National Board standards in his teaching practice.

Taking responsibility: Underwood took responsibility for his own learning and that of his students when he implemented an idea (having students show their understanding of science concepts through drawing) that was triggered by one of his NBPTS entries.

Communicating a vision: Nichols communicated a vision for her critical friends group when she outlined the steps of the protocol before the discussion started.

These are some of the key ways in which the teachers in the study exhibited leadership in professional growth experiences. Significantly, in each of these examples, the teachers took on roles not always associated with teaching that therefore required a degree of risk, which relates to an idea discussed earlier about the importance of a culture of trust.

The Role of Administration

The tendency for the teachers in the study to take on leadership roles in professional growth instances is not to say that other educational leaders didn't play vital roles in teachers' reflection. Indeed, they did. In some of the most memorable cases of reflection, administrators were directly responsible for arranging the conditions and activities that made the teachers' reflection possible. For example, the adoption of the critical friends group was initiated by a principal. Likewise, Green's trip to the mathematics conference was supported by the school structures, which gave her time and money to attend. The difference here is that, in these cases, the administrators worried about the details and arrangements at the structural level and the teachers took leadership in the arenas of their own learning. When administrators directed the learning, as in Underwood's department meetings about state standards, the reflection seemed removed from the teachers' experience and less personally meaningful. When teachers had to take responsibility for organizational issues, as in King's pilot evaluation meetings, they had little time left for reflection. Both teachers and administrators play leadership roles, but those roles should be carefully delineated to support the most effective experiences possible.

The preceding sections on vision, commitment, developmental appropriateness, culture, leadership, and the role of administration provide a rough description of what made the teachers' most successful learning experiences with reflection so noticeably different from the other cases studied in the research.

CONCLUSION

The cases described in this book were selected to contribute to a better understanding of the role of reflection in teaching as experienced by four accomplished teachers in the various contexts of their practice. This perspective contributes to an understanding of the issues and intricacies of fostering reflective practice. Because reflection is so central to teacher learning and effective teaching (Hawley & Valli, 1999), the results of this study have implications for the professional learning of teachers—particularly in the current climate of change.

Recent developments in the literature on professional development reveal an increasing emphasis on the importance of reflection, leading to a host of new ideas for teacher learning that place reflection at the center. These ideas create more hope for effective teacher learning than do those that have been tried in the past, especially given the consistent agreement among researchers that, for too long, teachers' professional development has been disjointed, haphazard, inconsistent, and ineffectual (Hargreaves, 1997). However, for the new images to succeed, more attention must be paid to what makes for the most valuable professional growth experiences. Without considering teachers' perceptions of which efforts most significantly impact teaching and learning, it may be that the new ideas will suffer the same limitations as those in the past. In a time when educators and policy makers are recognizing the vital importance of quality teaching for student learning, continuing to "develop" teachers in outdated ways is ironic at best and counterproductive at worst.

Fortunately, teacher educators in large numbers are calling for a new paradigm of professional development—one that is ongoing, contextualized, and rooted in practice (Darling-Hammond & Sykes, 1999). Being so closely tied to teachers' practice, this new paradigm signals the importance of emphasizing teachers' agency in designing and guiding their own learning. Accordingly, opportunities for growth and development being proposed are more suited to the actual processes of teaching, including the capacity for reflection—the drawing of meaning from one's own experiences that helps teachers understand what they are doing and why, so as to continually improve teaching and learning.

In essence, a new vision has emerged for teachers' professional learning, one that moves away from failed efforts to "reform" teachers and toward activities that support and encourage them to be reflective about their practice. For policy makers and educators searching for ways to improve the quality of teaching, one of the best ways to do so may simply be to provide opportunities for teachers to reflect on their practice in meaningful ways that help them do their jobs well.

But the potential for learning associated with a reflective approach to practice depends on the opportunities available for teachers to engage in reflective activities—activities that require appropriate conditions and the resources to create them. Studying teachers' perspectives on the role of reflection as we have done in this book is a step forward in discovering the nature of those opportunities, their conditions, and their contribution to teaching and learning. The teachers' expert opinions on the subject of reflection in the various contexts of their lives reveal what is needed to make reflective teaching the practiced as well as the theoretical heart of "the learning profession." In this book, the teachers agreed that most effective reflection depends on the belief that, given the support and encouragement to do so, teachers can and do take on the toughest issues of teaching, using their senses of professional responsibility, their minds, and their hearts to focus squarely on issues of student learning. And after all, when it comes to effective education, that's what really matters.

References

Abbot, E. A. (1953). *Flatland: A romance of many dimensions.* New York: Dover.

Applebee, A. N., & Langer, J. A. (1983). Instructional scaffolding: Reading and writing as natural language activities. *Language Arts, 60*(2), 168–175.

Ball, D. L., & Cohen, D. K. (1999). Developing practice, developing practitioners: Toward a theory of professional education. In L. Darling-Hammond & G. Sykes (Eds.), *Teaching as the learning profession: Handbook of policy and practice.* San Francisco: Jossey-Bass.

Barth, R. S. (2001). *Learning by heart.* San Francisco: Jossey-Bass.

Berliner, D. C. (1988). *The development of expertise in pedagogy.* Paper presented at the Annual Meeting of the American Association of Colleges for Teacher Education, New Orleans.

Bloom, B. S. (Ed.). (1956). *Taxonomy of educational objectives: The classification of educational goals: Handbook I, cognitive domain.* New York: Longmans, Green.

Carter, K. (1993). The place of story in the study of teaching and teacher education. *Educational Researcher, 22*(1), 5-12, 18.

Clandinin, D. J. (1986). Rhythms in teaching: The narrative study of teachers' personal practical knowledge of classrooms. *Teaching and Teacher Education, 2* (4), 377–387.

Coalition of Essential Schools (December, 2001). *Critical Friends Groups.* Retrieved December 13, 2001, from http://www.cesnorthwest.org/critical_friends_groups.htm.

Collier, S. T. (1999). Characteristics of reflective thought during the student teaching experience. *Journal of Teacher Education, 50* (3), 173–181.

Danielson, C. (1996). *Enhancing professional practice: A framework for teaching.* Alexandria, VA: Association for Supervision and Curriculum Development.

Darling-Hammond, L. (1998). Teacher learning that supports student learning. *Educational Leadership, 55* (5), 6–11.

Darling-Hammond, L., & McLaughlin, M. (1995). Policies that support professional development in an era of reform. *Phi Delta Kappan, 76* (8), 597–604.

Darling-Hammond, L., & Sykes, G. (Eds.). (1999). *Teaching as the learning profession: Handbook of policy and practice.* San Francisco: Jossey-Bass.

Dewey, J. (1910). *How we think.* Mineola, NY: Dover.

Dewey, J. (1933). *How we think: A restatement of the relation of reflective thinking to the educative process.* Boston: Heath.

Erickson, F. (1985). *Qualitative methods in research on teaching* (Occasional Paper No. 81). East Lansing, MI: Michigan State University, Institute for Research on Teaching.

Ericsson, K., & Simon, H. (1980). Verbal reports as data. *Psychological Review, 87* (3), 215–251.

Fullan, M. G. (1991). *The new meaning of educational change.* New York: Teachers College Press.

Fullan, M. G., & Miles, M. B. (1992). Getting reform right: What works and what doesn't. *Phi Delta Kappan, 73* (10), 744–752.

Gardner, H. (2000). *The disciplined mind: Beyond facts and standardized tests, the K-12 Education That Every Child Deserves.* New York: Penguin.

Ginsburg, H. (1981). The clinical interview in psychological research on mathematical thinking: Aims, rationales, and techniques. *For the Learning of Mathematics, 1,* 4–11.

Goodson, I. F. (1997). Representing teachers. *Teaching and Teacher Education, 13* (1), 111–117.

Grimmett, P. P., MacKinnon, A. M., Erickson, G. L., & Riecken, T. J. (1990). Reflective practice in teacher education: An analysis of issues and programs. In R. T. Clift, W. R. Houston, & M. C. Pugach (Eds.), *Encouraging reflective practice in education: An analysis of issues and programs* (pp. 20–36). New York: Teachers College Press.

Grossman, P. L. (1989). A study in contrast: Sources of pedagogical content knowledge for secondary English. *Journal of Teacher Education, 40* (5), 24–31.

Grossman, P., and Shulman, L. (1994). Knowing, believing, and the teaching of English. In *Teachers thinking, teachers knowing.* Urbana, IL: National Council of Teachers of English.

Hammersley, M., & Atkinson, P. (1995). *Ethnography: Principles in practice* (2d ed.). London: Routledge.

Hargreaves, A. (1997). *Rethinking educational change with heart and mind.* Alexandria, VA: Association for Supervision and Curriculum Development.

Hawley, W. D., & Valli, L. (1999). The essentials of effective professional development. In L. Darling-Hammond & G. Sykes (Eds.), *Teaching as the learning profession: Handbook of policy and practice* (pp. 127–150). San Francisco: Jossey-Bass.

Hess, D. (1999). *Developing a typology for teaching preservice students to reflect: A case of curriculum deliberation.* Paper presented at the Annual Conference of the American Educational Research Association, Montreal.

Hill, P. T., Pierce, L. C., & Guthrie, J. W. (1997). *Reinventing public education.* Chicago: University of Chicago Press.

Hofstadter, D. R. (1979). *Gödel, Escher, Bach: An eternal golden braid.* New York: Basic.

Huberman, A. M., & Miles, M. B. (1992). Data management and analysis methods. In M. D. LeCompte, W. L. Millroy, & J. Preissle (Eds.), *Handbook of qualitative research in education* (pp. 428–444). San Diego: Academic.

Ingvarson, L. (1998). Professional development as the pursuit of professional standards: The standards based professional development systems. *Teaching and Teacher Education, 14* (1), 127–140.

Intrator, S. M. (2002). *Stories of the courage to teach: Honoring the teacher's heart.* San Francisco: Jossey-Bass.

Jay, J. K. (2001). *Matters of reflection in quality teaching: A study of teachers' reflection in the contexts of their professional lives.* Unpublished doctoral dissertation, University of Washington, Seattle.

Jay, J. K. (2002). Points on a continuum: An expert/novice study of pedagogical reasoning. *The Professional Educator, 24* (2), 63–74.

Jay, J. K., & Johnson, K. L. (2002). Capturing complexity: A review and typology of reflective practice. *Teaching and Teacher Education, 18* (1), 73–85.

Jenkins, K. (2000). Earning board certification: Making time to grow. *Educational Leadership, 57* (8), 46–48.

Kane, C. M. (1994). *Prisoners of time: Research: What we know and what we need to know* (EA026453). Washington, D.C.: National Education Commission on Time and Learning.

Killion, J. P., & Todnem, G. R. (1991). A process for personal theory building. *Educational Leadership, 43* (6), 14–16.

Kouzes, J. M., & Posner, B. Z. (1999). *Encouraging the heart: A leader's guide to rewarding and recognizing others.* San Francisco: Jossey-Bass.

Ladson-Billings, G. (1999). Preparing teachers for diversity. In L. Darling-Hammond & G. Sykes (Eds.), *Teaching as the learning profession.* San Francisco: Jossey-Bass.

Langer, J. A., & Applebee, A. N. (1986). Reading and writing instruction: Toward a theory of teaching and learning. *Review of Research in Education, 13*, 171–194.

Lortie, D. (1975). *Schoolteacher: A sociological study.* Chicago: University of Chicago Press.

Loughran, J. (April, 1995). *Windows into the thinking of an experienced teacher: Exploring the influence of spontaneous "talk aloud" in practice.* Paper presented at the Annual Meeting of the American Educational Research Association, San Francisco.

Mahaley, D. (1999). One teacher's account. *The Clearing House, 73* (1), 5.

McKenna, H. (1999). *A pedagogy of reflection: Pathfinding in a time of change.* Paper presented at the Annual Conference of the American Association of Colleges of Teacher Education, Washington, D.C.

Miles, M. B., & Huberman, A. M. (1994). *Qualitative data analysis.* London: Sage.

Munby, H., & Russell, T. (1990). Metaphor in the study of teachers' professional knowledge. *Theory into Practice, 29* (2), 116–121.

National Board for Professional Teaching Standards (January, 2001). *National Board for Professional Teaching Standards.* Retrieved January 18, 2001, from World Wide Web: http://www.nbpts.org.

Noddings, N. (1986). Fidelity in teaching, teacher education, and research for teaching. *Harvard Educational Review, 56*, 496–510.

Ochs, E. (1997). Narrative. In T. V. Dijk (Ed.), *Discourse as structure and process* (pp. 185–207). Newbury Park, CA: Sage.

Palmer, P. J. (1997). The heart of a teacher: Identity and integrity in teaching. *Change, 29* (6), 14–22.

Palmer, P. J. (1998). *The courage to teach.* San Francisco: Jossey-Bass.

Patton, M. Q. (1980). Qualitative interviewing. In M. Q. Patton (Ed.), *Qualitative evaluation methods* (pp. 195–263). Beverly Hills, CA: Sage.

Polanyi, L. (1985). *Telling the American story: A structural and cultural analysis of conversational storytelling.* Norwood, NJ: Ablex.

Pressley, M., & Afflerbach, P. (1995). *Verbal reports of reading: The nature of constructively responsive reading.* Hillsdale, NJ: Erlbaum.

Richert, A. E. (1990). Teaching teachers to reflect: A consideration of programme structure. *Journal of Curriculum Studies, 22* (6), 509–527.

Sarason, S. B. (1990). *The predictable failure of educational reform.* San Francisco: Jossey-Bass.

Sarason, S. (1996). *Revisiting the culture of the school and the problem of change.* New York: Teachers College Press.

Sarason, S. B. (1996). *The culture of the school and the problem of change* (2nd Ed.). New York: Teachers College Press.

Schön, D. (1983). *The reflective practitioner: How professionals think in action.* New York: Basic.

Schön, D. A. (1987). *Educating the reflective practitioner: Toward a new design for teaching and learning in the profession.* San Francisco: Jossey-Bass.

Senge, P. M. (1990). *The fifth discipline: The art and practice of the learning organization.* New York: Currency Doubleday.

Shulman, L. S. (1987). Knowledge and teaching: Foundations of the new reform. *Harvard Educational Review, 57* (1), 1–21.

Sizer, T. R., & Sizer, N. F. (1999). *The students are watching: Schools and the moral contract.* Boston: Beacon.

Smylie, M. A. (1995). Teacher learning in the workplace: Implications for school reform. In T. R. Guskey & M. Humberman (Eds.), *Professional development in education: New paradigms and practices.* New York: Teachers College Press.

Strauss, A. (1987). *Qualitative analysis for social scientists.* Cambridge: Cambridge University Press.

Swain, L. (1999). You can't be a quitter: An account of achieving National Board Certification. *Teaching and Change, 6* (4), 409–415.

Valli, L. (1997). Listening to other voices: A description of teacher reflection in the United States. *Peabody Journal of Education, 72* (1), 67–88.

Van Manen, M. (1977). Linking ways of knowing with ways of being practical. *Curriculum Inquiry, 6*, 205–228.

Wildman, T. M., Magliaro, S. G., Niles, J. A., & McLaughlin, R. A. (1990). Promoting reflective practice among beginning and experienced teachers. In R. T. Clift, W. R. Houston, & M. C. Pugach (Eds.), *Encouraging reflective practice in education: An analysis of issues and programs* (pp. 139–161). New York: Teachers College Press.

Wolf, K. (1994). Teaching portfolios: Capturing the complexity of teaching. In L. Ingvarson & R. Chadbourne (Eds.), *Valuing teachers' work: New directions in teacher appraisal.* Victoria, Australia: Australian Council for Educational Research.

Zeichner, K. M. (1994). Conceptions of reflective practice in teaching and teacher education. In G. Harvard & P. Hodkinson (Eds.), *Action and reflection in teacher education.* Norwood, NJ: Ablex.

Index

academic, 16, 21, 29, 137, 147
academic tradition. *See* traditions of
  educational reform
accountability, 96, 113
activity, 3, 5, 7, 10, 12, 14, 17–23, 25–29,
  32–33, 35–57, 53–56, 72, 76, 80, 81,
  83, 87–91, 92, 100, 102, 104, 106, 107,
  108, 109, 112, 113, 115, 116, 117, 120,
  125, 127, 129, 132–37, 139, 141, 143,
  144, 146, 151–55, 157, 158, 160–61,
  163, 165, 167, 170–77, 178–92, 195,
  197, 198, 201, 202; dimensions of,
  26–27; facilitated, 26, 29, 31; naturally
  occurring, 26, 29, 31, 133;
  nonreflective, 33, 53, 64, 83, 88, 89,
  116 (*see also* nonreflective); reflective,
  4, 5, 14, 17–22, 26–28, 30, 31, 33, 40,
  48, 50, 56, 62, 67, 68, 83, 104, 105,
  106, 116, 125, 137, 138–39, 156–59,
  166, 168, 171, 175, 176, 181, 184, 185,
  187, 188, 190, 192, 193, 198, 200, 203
  (*see also* reflective); structured, 19, 31,
  36, 54, 55, 59, 75, 86, 89, 90, 135–37,
  156, 166 (*see also* structure)
administration, 88, 116, 201. *See also*
  leadership
administrative, 20, 53, 54, 57, 66, 71, 90,
  134; activities, 181; agenda, 57; details,
  118; items, 56; matters, 114; needs, 71,
  118; support, 190; tasks, 116, 134, 167,
  186
administrator, 26, 41, 43–48, 50, 51, 54,
  55, 57, 59, 63, 66–69, 75, 87, 89, 117,
  131, 137, 141, 166, 180, 181, 189, 190,

191, 193, 196, 197, 201. *See also*
  leaders; leadership
affective, 140, 164, 172
after school, 31, 77, 81, 113, 128, 178,
  186, 200
agenda, 42–47, 51, 53, 56–59, 88, 146,
  148, 166, 179. *See also* meeting;
  department meeting, competing
  agendas in
analysis, 17, 184–85, 190, 196;
  curriculum, 14; data, 32–34; of
  practice, 19, 88, 106–8, 184; of student
  work, 19, 106–7, 184. *See also*
  National Board; portfolio; standards;
  student work
assessment, 8, 27, 37, 58, 94, 111–13, 118,
  133, 135, 137–38; high-stakes, 112,
  117; of lessons, 175; self-, 54, 116,
  118; state, 54–55; teacher, 31, 91–94,
  97, 112–18, 126, 134–35, 137–38, 157,
  170, 173, 175, 177–78, 180–81,
  185–86; voluntary, 113–18. *See also*
  evaluation; programs

barriers. *See* reflection, barriers to
bonus, 129–32
break: Christmas, 128; in a day, 128;
  spring, 128; summer, 171. *See also*
  vacation
bureaucratic, 20; structure, 51, 91

case, 5–6, 9–10, 24–34, 37–38, 40, 62, 71,
  83, 86, 89, 92–95, 99, 127–28, 132–33,
  138–41, 171–77, 178–79, 181–88, 190,

192–97, 199, 201; of conversations with colleagues, 147–50, 150–58; from a critical friends group, 142–51; of department meetings, 51–59; of informal collegial meetings, 60–65; learning from, 38, 93, 139; of a lunchtime study group, 60–62; of mentoring programs, 119–26; from the National Board Certification process, 100–12; of reflection in the context of teaching, 74–82; from a regional conference, 152–62; of staff meetings, 41–48; of teacher evaluation, 66–73; of teachers' experience, 23, 40, 97, 179; from teachers' individualized activities, 163–69; of a voluntary program for teacher assessment, 113–18

case study, 5, 23, 24–34. *See also* research
certification. *See* National Board for Professional Teaching Standards, certification

climate, 31, 33, 50, 193; emotional, 199; of change, 202; of competition, 21. *See also* culture

Coalition of Essential Schools, 142

collaborate/collaboration, 21, 46, 65, 123, 122, 140

collaborative, 115, 164, 174; activities, 115; community, 142; conversation, 116, 124; culture of, 116; environment, 61, 65; groups, 47; structure, 115

collegial: communities, 173; contact, 86; groups, 89, 174–75; conversations, 186; meetings, 36, 59, 60–65, 66, 77, 83, 148 (*see also* meetings); reflection, 78, 158; relationships, 27, 78, 172. *See also* conversations, with colleagues; cases, of informal collegial meetings; network of colleagues; study group

collegiality, 150, 172, 190

colleague-to-colleague mentoring. *See* mentoring, peer helper relationship

commentary. *See* written commentary

community, 91, 94, 139, 140–41, 142, 146, 151, 153, 155, 176

comparative reflection. *See* reflection, comparative

conditions, 9, 12, 25–26, 27, 30, 33, 79, 112, 117, 121, 168, 190, 191, 198, 201,

203; classroom, 65; effects of, 20; for reflecting on one's own, 170–77; of context, 32; of programs, 127–37; of schools, 20, 76, 83–91; of teaching, 20, 82; supporting reflection, 10, 18, 37, 178–79, 189, 191–92

conference, 138, 140, 166, 168, 169, 170, 174, 176; mathematics, 7, 141, 151, 171–72, 188, 199, 201; parent, 166; regional, 152–62, 178; session, 182, 186; settings, 175; social aspects of, 182, 186

context, 9, 15, 33, 34, 41, 60, 72, 113, 115, 124, 125, 126, 150, 159, 160, 164, 166, 170, 201, 203; across, 178–94; dimensions of, 27; overarching, 33; personal, 138–41, 170, 171, 173, 174, 175, 176, 177, 178, 179, 181–82, 187, 188, 189, 193; professional, 35–40, 83, 90–91, 170–77, 178, 179–80, 181, 183, 186, 187, 188, 189; programmatic/of programs, 92–98, 127–37, 160, 170, 177, 178, 179, 180–81, 189; of reflection, 16, 20–21; school, 9, 48, 84–85, 87, 88, 90–91, 152, 155; of teaching, 14, 15, 19–20, 73, 74–82, 83. *See also* reflection

contextual factors, 33

conversations, 8, 31, 44, 49, 53, 79, 91, 125, 136, 140, 143, 155, 174, 178, 180, 186; with colleagues, 19, 77, 78, 79 87, 88, 155, 186, 189, 199. *See also* cases, of conversations with colleagues

cooperating teacher, 7, 8, 119–23, 186, 200. *See also* mentoring, cooperating teacher perspective on

cost, 108, 111, 113, 132, 136. *See also* emotional, toll

critical friends: conversations in, 143–50; groups, 30–31, 138, 141, 142–51, 152, 153, 155, 156, 159, 160, 170, 171, 174, 176, 178, 186, 188, 190, 178, 196–97, 199, 201; ideal, 142; meetings, 141, 142–46, 149, 150, 168–69, 186 (*see also* meetings); protocol, 143–46, 182. *See also* cases, from a critical friends group

critical reflection. *See* reflection, critical

culture, 8, 21, 27, 31, 32, 90, 91, 136, 174, 175, 193, 194, 199–200, 201; of

collaboration, 116; of schools, 21, 124, 126; of trust, 91, 150. *See also* climate
curriculum analysis. *See* analysis, curriculum

data, 29, 30, 191, 183; analysis (*see* analysis, data); displays, 33; preparation, 32; sources, 28, 30–32. *See also* interview; observation; research; stimulated recall
deliberative reflection. *See* reflection, deliberative
department, 6, 7, 49, 77, 78, 84, 89, 128, 129, 130, 140, 149, 156, 197; chair, 8, 189; goals, 180, 191; meetings, 20, 50–59, 60, 61, 66, 67, 76, 83, 88, 89, 124, 125, 156, 158, 159, 175, 180, 186, 187, 190, 201. *See also* meetings; agenda; cases, of department meetings
descriptive reflection. *See* reflection, descriptive
developmentalist tradition. *See* traditions of educational reform

emotional: abuse, 43; climate, 199; commitment, 138; current, 141; response, 157; toll, 136, 147. *See also* affective; cost
encourage/encouragement, 27, 58, 69, 70, 85, 86, 87, 88, 93, 104, 114, 115, 117, 127, 128, 131, 132, 136, 137, 140, 148, 156, 158, 159, 160, 170, 171, 180, 181, 188, 189, 191 196, 197, 198, 202, 203
Enhancing Professional Practice, 95, 113–17. *See also* professional
equity, 15, 16, 25, 35
evaluation, 27, 39, 88, 94, 114, 117, 133, 134, 197, 201; of practice, 19; teacher, 36, 65, 66–73, 74, 83, 89, 95, 113–14, 127, 129, 160, 186, 187; self-evaluation, 1. *See also* assessment; observation

facilitated activities. *See* activities, facilitated
financial bonus. *See* bonus
foster, fostering. *See* reflection, fostering
framework, 16, 36, 38, 92, 93, 116, 135, 167, 139

generic tradition. *See* traditions of educational reform
goal. *See* reflection, goal of
Green, Ivy, 7, 38, 40, 51–53, 74–77, 81, 84, 85, 86, 87, 91, 92, 97, 100, 104, 105, 106, 108–11, 129, 130, 131, 134, 140, 151, 152–62, 171, 175, 176, 179, 183, 188, 189, 190, 192, 197, 198, 199, 200, 201

heart, 137, 138, 146, 148, 151, 170, 177; of quality teaching, 2, 195–203
high-stakes, 35, 97, 112, 113, 117

instruction, 14, 26, 64, 65, 71, 74, 79, 80, 108, 165; critiquing, 26; in the midst of, 74, 75, 77, 81, 186; time, 46
instructional: act, 67; approaches, 54; effectiveness, 46; practice, 194; strategies, 26; 52, 57; style, 19; tasks, 198. *See also* pedagogy
interviews/interviewing, 19, 29, 24, 30–31, 32, 34. *See also* research; data
intentionality, 189–91, 192
isolated/isolating, 146, 150, 193
isolation, 20, 21; student, 47; of teaching, 86

journal, 32, 45, 144, 165–66
journaling/journal writing, 19, 26, 61, 186

King, Mary, 8–9, 38, 39, 40, 54–59, 66–69, 74, 75, 76, 85, 86, 87, 91, 93, 97, 100, 105–7, 109, 111, 113–18, 129, 130, 131, 132, 133, 134, 140, 152, 163–65, 171, 180, 181, 189, 190, 191, 197, 199, 200, 201

leader, 6, 8, 22, 44
leadership, 51, 116, 174, 176, 188, 196, 200–1. *See also* administration; administrator
lunchtime study group. *See* study group; cases, of a lunchtime study group

materials, 26, 28, 32, 33, 35, 91, 99, 100, 106, 114, 115, 116, 117, 135, 142, 145, 192, 193, 181

meetings, 27, 29, 31, 33, 74, 79, 97, 99,
110, 111, 114, 115, 116, 117, 129, 136,
141, 152, 156, 163, 165, 166, 170, 174,
178, 180, 187, 188, 192, 197, 201. *See
also* agenda; collegial meetings;
department meetings; staff meetings;
critical friends groups
mentor, 7, 8, 128, 130, 134, 135
mentoring, 6, 8, 27, 136, 157, 176, 190;
cooperating teacher perspective on,
122–23; peer helper relationship,
123–25, 136, 186; programs 20, 30, 31,
93, 97, 119–26, 127, 129, 132, 178,
181, 190; student teacher perspective
on, 120–22. *See also* programs
metareflection. *See* reflection, meta-
money, 9, 27, 45, 58, 128, 132, 155, 172,
187, 201. *See also* resources
motivate, 44, 76, 100, 102, 106, 128, 129,
123, 176, 177,149, 156, 160, 174, 185,
188, 193, 194, 196
motivation, 90, 91, 117, 122, 127, 128,
129, 130, 140, 177, 189, 196, 200

National Board, 9, 18, 28, 29, 30, 93, 95,
97, 98, 99–112, 115, 129, 130, 132,
134, 135, 156, 157, 165, 176, 177, 178,
180, 190; candidates, 131, 134;
certified teachers, 6, 200; certification,
7, 95, 123, 129, 130, 131, 140, 190,
199; facilitation, 131; mission, 99;
process, 97, 113, 116, 117, 126, 128,
130, 132, 136, 159; risk of applying,
130; standards, 129, 200. *See also*
analysis, of student work; portfolio;
professional; programs; standards,
reflecting on; videotape
National Board for Professional Teaching
Standards. *See* National Board
naturally occurring activities. *See*
activities, naturally occurring
NBPTS. *See* National Board for
Professional Teaching Standards
network, 20, 155, 157; of colleagues,
62–65
Nichols, Laura, 8–9, 39, 60–62, 65, 74, 77,
85, 89, 91, 92, 97, 100, 102, 107, 111,
122–26, 128, 129, 130, 133, 134, 136,
140, 142–51, 152, 153, 156, 160,

165–67, 171, 172, 174, 181, 183, 188,
189, 190, 192, 196, 198, 199, 200
nonreflective, 74, 104, 106, 109, 115, 118,
166, 172, 173, 174, 181, 182, 186–88,
194. *See also* activity, nonreflective

observation, 30–31, 32, 33, 69, 120, 122,
123, 124, 154; classroom, 67–69; peer,
19. *See also* evaluation; research; data
organizational structure. *See* structure,
organizational
overload, 31, 35

pedagogical reasoning, 14
pedagogy, 126, 103, 181. *See also*
instructional
peer helper. *See* mentoring, peer helper
relationship
peer observation. *See* observation, peer
peer review, 20
personal: challenge, 130; connection, 199;
development, 199; gains, 25, 27; goals,
116; growth, 15; interest, 130, 167,
177; places, 163–69; preferences, 171;
standards, 96; time, 91, 187
personal context. *See* context, personal
personalistic reflection. *See* reflection,
personalistic
pilot. *See* evaluation
policy, 62; district policy, 62–65, 51–54;
school policy, 147
policymakers, 2, 5, 41, 202
portfolio, 31, 32, 96, 97, 105–12, 118, 128,
186; creation, 19, 26, 29; directions, 31;
entries, 33. *See also* analysis, of student
work; National Board; standards;
videotape; written commentary
professional context. *See* context,
professional
professional: activities, 5, 20, 157,
176–77; advancement, 157;
development, 5, 6, 8, 27, 31, 91, 202;
gain, 25; goal, 72, 73; growth, 6,
69–71, 72, 93–94, 113, 176, 186,
195–202, 201; learning, 2, 35, 176,
202; judgment, 3; opportunities, 129,
130–31; risk, 86, 136, 201; wisdom, 4.
See also Enhancing Professional
Practice; National Board; teacher

programs, 5, 8, 20, 27, 29, 31, 897, 91, 92–98, 112, 116, 127–37, 138, 139, 141, 160, 168, 170, 172, 176, 181, 184, 188, 189, 190, 193, 195. *See also* assessment, teacher; assessment, voluntary programs for; mentoring; National Board
programmatic context. *See* context, programmatic
propositions, 33. *See also* research
protocol. *See* critical friends group, protocol
puzzle of practice, 75–77, 79–81, 88, 120, 144–45, 184, 199

questions, 2, 3, 8, 17, 19, 20, 21, 24, 30, 41, 51, 54, 58, 59, 62, 63, 65, 67, 72, 75, 81, 90, 91, 94, 95, 97, 106, 113, 117, 122, 123, 132, 144, 148, 149, 150, 156, 165, 166, 183, 184; for analyzing reflection, 17, 36–38, 98, 120, 139, 141; to guide reflection, 27, 45, 47, 57, 100, 103, 120, 121, 122, 133, 135, 137, 144, 145, 148, 155, 157, 159, 181; research. *See* research, questions
reflective. *See* reflective, questions
quality teaching, 2–6, 9, 17, 22, 26, 65, 76, 79, 86, 87, 116, 122, 170, 187–94, 195–203

recognition, 110, 128, 129, 130–31, 195
reflection: barriers to, 2, 179, 188–94; benefits of, 4, 11, 22, 34, 170, 171–72; boosts for, 127, 179, 188–94; challenges of, 91, 127, 170, 171–72; comparative, 18; content of, 16, 33, 35; context of (*see* context, of reflection); critical, 18; cycle of, 13–14; definition of, 11–14, 23, 38–39, 66, 78, 95–96, 98, 145, 178; descriptive, 18; deliberative, 15; dimensions of, 25, 26, 34; effective, 2, 18, 64, 82, 133, 173, 203; -for-action, 10, 12–13; foster/fostering, 4, 5, 17, 18, 46, 57, 72, 78, 76, 98, 104, 113, 136, 137, 142, 150, 173–74; goal of, 25, 26, 27, 33; -in-action, 12–13, 14; key concepts, 25–28; importance of, 3, 9, 39, 140, 202; invisibility of, 145; meta-, 22; nature of, 38–49, 133, 139, 178; -

on-action, 12–13, 14; personalistic, 15; process of, 17, 25–26, 33; purpose of, 18–19, 150; quality of, 16, 17–18, 22, 149, 176–76, 179, 182–88; risk of, 86; standards-based, 96, 112; studying, 24–34; teachers' perspectives on, 14–15, 21–22, 138, 178; technical, 15–16; types of, 15–17; value of, 23, 150, 179, 182–88; varieties of, 14–15, 17, 18, 21, 23, 27. *See also* activities; context
reflective: experiences, 21, 27, 28, 33, 65, 88, 119, 160, 166, 169, 172, 174, 178, 188, 198; opportunities, 33, 60, 72, 91, 115, 118, 148, 173, 179, 180, 181, 182, 185, 188; practice, 2, 3, 4, 5, 6, 9, 11, 16, 17, 25, 30, 48, 86, 112, 120, 121, 127, 128, 134, 167, 174, 192, 202; questions, 19, 43, 52, 126, 160. *See also* activity, reflective
reflectivity, 28, 29; levels of, 15
regional conference. *See* cases, from a regional conference
research, 2–10, 35, 38, 39, 41, 44, 70, 71, 92, 178, 182, 183, 184, 188, 191, 193, 196, 198, 201, 202; consensus in, 2–3; methods, 24–34; on reflection, 11–23, 70, 179; questions, 9–10, 24–25, 28. *See also* case study; data; interviews; observation; propositions
resources, 19, 21, 42, 52, 90, 142, 161, 174, 188, 203. *See also* money

schedule, 35, 76, 78, 84, 128, 147, 168. *See also* time
school-based reflection. *See* context, professional
schools. *See* culture, of schools; structure, of schools
self-assessment. *See* assessment, self-
self-evaluation. *See* evaluation, self-
social efficiency. *See* traditions of educational reform
social reconstructivist. *See* traditions of educational reform
staff meetings. *See* cases, of staff meetings
standards, 15, 19, 27, 29, 30, 54, 96, 112, 113, 115, 116, 129, 130, 133, 135, 137, 144, 186, 196, 197, 200; external, 96,

98; internal, 96; personal 96; reflecting on, 186; school, 76; state, 115, 190. *See also* analysis, of practice

stimulated recall, 32. *See also* data; research

stress, 20, 48, 137, 169

structure, 27, 31, 44, 47, 48, 51, 52, 53, 72, 76, 81, 84, 85, 90–91, 103, 112, 113, 114, 125, 126, 128, 135, 136, 137, 141, 143, 144, 145, 148, 149, 157, 166, 168, 171, 174, 176, 177, 179, 180, 181, 183, 184, 188, 189, 193; educational, 173; organizational, 20, 68; power, 20; of schools, 4, 20, 21, 31, 86, 175, 179, 193, 194, 201. *See also* activity, structured

student: achievement, 35; apathy, 149; engagement, 26; evaluations, 71–72; input, 185; learning, 2, 17, 25, 48, 51, 52, 54, 56, 67, 68, 67, 77, 103, 107, 109, 110, 133, 144, 157, 161, 176, 185, 187, 190, 196, 197, 202, 203; participation, 54, 147; teacher, 42, 60, 122–23, 124, 119–22, 126, 133, 134, 186, 190, 192, 193, 200; understanding, 107; work, 19, 26, 30, 31, 105–7, 112, 117, 135, 183, 186. *See also* analysis, of student work

study group, 89, 164, 175, 183, 189, 197. *See also* cases, of a lunchtime study group

teacher: accomplished, 1, 2, 4, 9, 10, 22, 24, 34, 76, 83, 95, 98, 112, 129, 157, 164, 179, 188, 201; development, 155; education, 8, 16, 123, 131; evaluation (*see* evaluation, teacher; cases, of teacher evaluation); leadership (*see* leader; leadership); learning, 3, 11, 20, 27, 34, 69, 91, 112, 116, 185, 195, 196, 202; perspectives, 27–28. *See also* professional

teacher assessment. *See* assessment, teacher; *Enhancing Professional Practice*; National Board; programs

technical, 160; application of knowledge, 15; approach to reflection, 16; aspects of portfolio creation, 186; issues, 104; knowledge, 15; matters, 116; requirements, 106; support, 115. *See also* administrative; reflection, technical

technician model of teaching, 92

time, 4, 7, 8, 9, 12, 21, 27, 30, 33, 35, 37, 38, 39, 40, 44, 45, 46, 47, 49, 84, 85, 87, 88, 89, 90, 91, 115, 116, 117, 119, 121, 122, 123, 136, 128, 131, 133, 134, 135, 138, 140, 144, 146, 148, 151, 154, 155, 156, 158, 159, 161, 162, 164, 166, 167, 168, 170, 172, 173, 174, 175, 176, 177, 178, 131, 180, 182, 139, 191, 192, 193, 194, 197, 201, 202. *See also* schedule

traditions of educational reform, 16

trust, 21, 64, 91, 123, 125, 126, 140, 145, 149, 150, 166, 173–74, 175, 199, 201

Underwood, Kirk, 6–7, 38, 39, 40, 41, 42–44, 45–48, 51, 62–65, 69–72, 75–79, 84, 85, 86, 87, 88, 91, 92, 96, 97, 100, 101–5, 106, 107, 109, 111, 128, 129, 131, 133, 140, 152, 156, 171, 175, 167–68, 180, 183, 192, 193, 197, 198, 199, 200, 201

vacation, 171. *See also* break

videotape, 19, 26, 29, 100, 101–5, 106, 108, 112, 133, 134, 135, 186. *See also* National Board

voluntary programs for teacher assessment. *See* assessment, teacher; cases, of a voluntary program for teacher assessment

wisdom of practice, 21, 22, 24

work overload. *See* overload

written commentary, 112. *See also* portfolio

About the Author

Joelle Jay is an educational consultant and coach with Pillar Consulting in Reno, Nevada. She facilitates workshops, meetings, and school-improvement projects for teachers and educational leaders. In addition to working with schools to improve teaching and learning, she serves as an adjunct professor at the University of Nevada, Reno. She has published several articles and other works on teachers' reflection. This is her first book.

Dr. Jay is a former researcher and associate at the Institute for K-12 Learning at the University of Washington. She also served as a facilitator and consultant with the Washington Initiative to Support National Board Candidates. In addition to teaching teachers and educational leaders, Jay taught ninth-grade English for several years.

Dr. Jay holds a Ph.D. in teacher education from the University of Washington, a master of arts degree in teaching from Boston University, and a bachelor of arts degree in education from the University of Nevada, Reno.